A *Lively* Connection

INTIMATE ENCOUNTERS WITH THE ETHICAL MOVEMENT IN AMERICA

Edited by
Cable Neuhaus

Ethica Press / THE PRESS OF THE
AMERICAN ETHICAL UNION
New York City

A LIVELY CONNECTION:
INTIMATE ENCOUNTERS WITH THE ETHICAL MOVEMENT IN AMERICA

EDITED BY CABLE NEUHAUS

Copyright © 1978 by Ethica Press
All rights reserved
First printing: September 1978

Published by: Ethica Press
      2 West 64th Street
      New York, New York 10023

ISBN 0-930732-02-2

Cover design by Sven Feyler
Manufactured in the United States of America

From whatever point we start, we arrive at the same conclusion still: "not in the creed but in the deed!" In the deed is the pledge of the sacredness of life; in the deed is the reward of our activities in health; in the deed our solace, and our salvation even in the abysmal gulfs of woe. In hours of great sorrow we turn in vain to nature for an inspiring thought. We question the sleepless stars; they are cold and distant; the winds blow, the rivers run their course, the seasons change: they are careless of man . . . . Let us grasp hands cordially and look into each other's eyes for sympathy, while we travel together on our road toward the unknown goal. To help one another is our wisdom, and our renown, and our sweet consolation.

> From *Creed and Deed* by FELIX ADLER, founder of the Ethical movement.

Without "ethical culture" there is no salvation for humanity.

> ALBERT EINSTEIN on the occasion of the Ethical movement's seventy-fifth anniversary, 1951.

TABLE OF CONTENTS

TABLE OF CONTENTS

PREFACE

MY FRIEND Fred Rogers, whose popular children's TV series *Mister Rogers' Neighborhood* has been on the air nearly as long as I have been alive, takes as his guiding philosophy the simple notion that "every person is special and each of us can make a difference in the world." It is an exquisite philosophy, I think, perfect in its sparkling humanity. And while it has plainly worked as a comforting thought for the millions of American pre-schoolers who have been raised, as it were, in Fred's gentle neighborhood, it could just as aptly be applied as a way of characterizing the focus of the essays collected in this volume. In spite of sometimes marked differences in backgrounds and specific orientations, all of the contributors here affirm their sense of extraordinary good fortune in being viable humans on the planet Earth.

Another bond — a superficial but practical one — which all of these contributors share is the domain of the Ethical movement in America. Whether self-identified as an Ethical Culturist or an Ethical humanist (or even, in one instance, an *existential* humanist), everyone congregated here has demonstrated a living commitment to the philosophical and religious vision of Felix Adler, whose "deed, not creed"-view of the world, first publicly pronounced by him in 1876, at once startled this nation's clergy and provided a welcomed outlet

7

for those who had grown disenchanted with, among other things, matters of liturgy.

A Lively Connection: Intimate Encounters with the Ethical Movement in America is intended as a kind of celebration in honor of the Ethical movement's centennial. That the ideals of Dr. Adler and his early associates have brought disparate peoples together for one hundred years is reason enough, surely, for thanksgiving. And, too, for stock-taking. Which is why these essays (most of which are by Ethical Leaders who are or once were ordained and thus qualifed to perform an assortment of typical pastoral duties) at times express varying judgments as to the direction of "Ethical" today. If the collection sometimes seems disharmonious it is because a pattern of what might well be called "creative tension" has long marked the movement — and has prompted countless of its adherents to acts of magnanimity and courageous persistence against all forms of human oppression.

It is not necessary to read these essays in the order in which they are presented. However, those who do will find that there is a natural flow to their sequence. The first several essays, led off by Ed Ericson's ranging inquiry into the need for ethical religion, take us swiftly to Ies Spetter's powerful evocation of death (and life) in Nazi-overrun Europe. This is followed immediately by the lovely and, in its own way, liberating, story, "Doug and Barbara," by Arthur Dobrin. "Jeff" Hornback, Khoren Arisian, and others then offer a variety of personal statements which underscore the value of the movement in their lives — lives which, it should be pointed out, have been quite diverse but uniformly marked by thoughtful action. The next group of essays center around the "spiritual" vs. the "scientifically objective" camps which have lately waged their cordial confrontation under the aegis of the American Ethical Union, the administrative agency which oversees the activities of the country's Ethical societies and fellowships. (Noteworthy is that among those who call for a return to "spirituality" is Jean Kotkin, the non-cleric executive director of the AEU.) The concluding essay, by the distinguished Columbia University philosophy professor Joseph Blau, serves not only as a wonderful summing up but also as a clarion call to all those who harbor doubts concerning the future of liberal religion. "It would be pretentious to say that the future lies entirely in our hands; we are too few for that," writes the impassioned scholar. "But we can at least serve to keep alive the gleam in an age of gloom."

Because the book which was published on the occasion of the Ethical movement's fiftieth anniversary included a substantial

8

amount of autobiographical material, the present volume in that respect follows its predecessor. These new essays, though, are not all-inclusive: that is to say, while they are representative of the thinking within the movement today, they certainly do not presume to serve as the final word (within "Ethical," it sometimes seems that there *is* no final word — regarding *anything*!). There are Leaders not included in this book whose ideas are stimulating and worthy of an audience but who, for one reason or another, were uncomfortable with the chore of writing about their own lives. And, as any reader will quickly discover, even those who accepted the invitation (and whose work was subsequently selected for publication) were not of like mind concerning how an autobiographical statement ought to be handled. In one or two instances the choice was not to handle it at all. (Modesty has a variety of ways of asserting itself, although it seemingly asserts itself seldom within the ranks of Ethical Leaders. This is not a disparagement; it is merely an observation that many Leaders themselves have deliberately brought to my attention.)

I like all of these essays, for each expresses thoughts, or glimmers of thoughts, which I too have entertained — but which I sometimes feared were not shared by others. *A Lively Connection* (the title is derived from Khoren Arisian's oft-expressed definition of the Ethical movement as "a lively connectedness with the world") comforts me; it assures me that there *is* a linkage, a network of people whose primary motivation in life is the cultivation in the human species of all the caring and affection and reason of which we are congenitally capable. What I read in these statements is an urgent request for less self-righteousness among Americans (although so-called born-again Christians may well have already cornered the market in that department) and a greater piety concerning all things of this earth. To again quote Fred Rogers (who, interestingly, is a Presbyterian minister): "Every person is special and each of us can make a difference in the world."

One has several objectives in mind when publishing a book of this sort. Primary, of course, is bringing to the attention of humanists everywhere the latest thinking about Ethical humanism *by* Ethical humanists. Another objective, as I noted earlier, is simply to celebrate the movement's passage into its second century. But perhaps just as important — maybe even more so — is the good such a collection can do in introducing this quiet little movement to those who have never heard of it. It is not a difficult thing to meander through an entire lifetime without ever being exposed to — critics might say *contaminated by* — the tenets of Ethical humanism. I personally knew virtually nothing about the movement until about five years ago when I happened upon a brief item about Humanist Manifesto II in a national publication and then undertook to find out what kind of people would dare to sign such an exceptionally rational document. It was a back-door route to "Ethical." *A Lively Connection* would have been a saner approach had it been readily available and known to me. I am therefore especially hopeful that young people will have an opportunity to read some of these selections. It is shameful that, in this age of skepticism about so many things, people under thirty (who so often throughout history have been in the vanguard of "human" movements) have not been properly introduced to Felix Adler's message. His remains an idea with a universality and a timelessness. It but needs a fuller airing in the public arena.

Finally, a word of thanks: In preparing this volume for publication I am indebted to a number of individuals of humanist convictions who assisted in the plethora of tedious tasks that are necessarily involved in such a project. Among those, Ies Spetter and Khoren Arisian were instrumental in persuading Ethica Press that this collection was worth putting between covers. And I am especially grateful to Arthur Dobrin, poet and Ethical Leader, whose enterprise and whose faith in me enabled *A Lively Connection* to ultimately come alive. His help cannot be overstated. This is the appropriate place, as well, to offer my gratitude to all those humanists, living and gone, whose lives have been like a candle . . . guiding my way and illuminating even my darkest days.

Pittsburgh, Pennsylvania   CABLE NEUHAUS
June 1978

INTRODUCTION:
ETHICAL VALUES AND HUMAN FAITH
WITHOUT DOGMA OR SECTARIANISM

Algernon D. Black

THE QUEST for a meaningful life free from superstition, the quest for a commitment to an ethical humanist faith, did not begin in 1876 with the founding by Felix Adler of the New York Society for Ethical Culture. Its roots are to be found in the dawn of conscience, in the open-ended dialectics of the ancient Greek philosophers, and also in the fiery denunciations of ritual and the call to righteousness by the Prophets of Israel. We can point to the quest for truth by Akhenaten in ancient Egypt and the insight and spirit of Jesus of Nazareth. And beyond our knowing, but surely real throughout human history, have been the countless unknown individuals in every tribe and village, in small nations and large, who have dared to think for themselves and question the dominant beliefs and moralities of their time and place.

The faith of the Enlightenment of the eighteenth century was based on the assumption that man was capable of reason, and could achieve a certain objectivity beyond appearances and beyond local prejudices. That faith expressed confidence that human beings could be free, could be disciplined by their own values, and could govern themselves individually and collectively. Those great spirits who articulated the themes of the Age of Reason were giving voice not merely to their own needs and aspirations; they were writing

11

and speaking for increasing numbers of human beings in Europe and America who sensed the potentialities in people and the possibility of a better life for all.

The Ethical movement was born of the philosophical and religious and moral climate of the last half of the nineteenth century. The continuing influence of rationalism and the spirit of the French and American Revolutions had been working in the minds of people in Europe and America. In Europe the year 1848 was marked by liberal movements for democratic constitutional government. The reaction drove many of the most independent and courageous leaders into prison or exile. Some made their way to the United States, where, in comparative political freedom, they found asylum. The spirit of freedom and of faith in the human were stimulated by the emergence of science, dramatized by Darwin's *Origin of Species*; they were fortified by the findings of archaeology and anthropology which furthered understanding of the history of man's intellectual and cultural development. The continuing impact of the Industrial Revolution and scientific technology on human conditions and relationships set the stage for criticism of institutions and values.

It was inevitable that traditional beliefs and assumptions should be threatened. When people questioned the legitimacy of kings, emperors, and hereditary aristocracies, traditional religious institutions were not exempt. Revolt against the authority of churches, temples, and hierarchical clergy was accompanied by the questioning of the creeds and myths, the rituals and miracles.

It was no accident that the Ethical movement emerged in 1876 and that the first Ethical Culture societies were founded in America. This was due to both the critical movements pervasive in the western world and the conditions in the United States. 1876 was the year in which Americans could celebrate the survival of the nation after the crisis of a bloody Civil War with victory for the Federal Union and freedom for the slaves. The atmosphere was one of optimism and change and diversity.

By the 1870s the nation was benefitting from the expansion to the west and the extraordinary productivity and material progress made possible by open land, plentiful raw materials, and a varied climate. The Atlantic Ocean had made it possible for the United States to prosper and develop its own institutions and its distinctive character. Two other factors played an extremely powerful part: the democratic ethic at the heart of the political structure and the character and motivation of the people who implemented the American way of life.

The ethic embodied in the Constitution provided for a structure of federal government and a process of decision-making. That the people of the colonies refused to ratify the Constitution without a Bill of Rights is evidence of their realism and wisdom. The first ten amendments providing for religious freedom, freedom of speech and press, and freedom of association, for fair trial and equal protection of the laws, gave promise of equality of rights and opportunities for all.

The federal system, based on national and local participation, with both concentration and decentralization of power, gave a means of achieving unity within a framework of diversity. The system of checks and balances offered some security against the over-concentration of power. The electoral process held out hope of popular choice of officials and accountability to the people.

Although the compromise with slavery and the denial of universal suffrage were violations of the principle of equality, remedies were available. When prejudices and vested interests repudiated the needs and aspirations of any individual or section of the population, the methods of decision-making could provide for obtaining "redress of grievances" — *if* the people were concerned and responsible. When issues and programs could not be adopted by the federal government because of conflicting interests or prejudices, states or local governments might lead the way. Then in good time a consensus might emerge, ready to solve the problems on a national level.

Thus the American people had an apparatus for decision-making by which they could fulfill the promises of freedom and equality for all. But the wisdom and the foresight of those who shaped the Constitution and a democratic ethic would have been fruitless if the people who came after lacked the ability to make their vision effective.

In the latter half of the nineteenth century the individuals and families who migrated to the United States from many lands brought their strengths and energies, their talents and skills, the capacity for hard work, their motivations to better themselves. Most of all, they brought great expectations. Many came with nothing, at great sacrifice of property in the lands of their birth. Whatever their religious, racial, and national backgrounds, they made a commitment to this land of opportunity and the democratic ethic. Despite the discrimination and exploitation and deprivation they encountered, their dream never died. If it was weakened or destroyed in the parents, it was reborn in the young.

13

It was to be expected that some people would hold tight to traditional institutions and ways of thinking, but the diversity of sects and denominations was bound to raise questions and doubts. The confrontation of differences in religious beliefs and practices was something never experienced in quite the same way in the "old country." If many clung to the past, there were also those who broadened in outlook and sought a new understanding of their own lives and the viewpoints of their neighbors. If the older generation held to traditional beliefs and identities, this was not necessarily true of their children, who studied, worked, and socialized with the children of their neighbors. With greater mobility and more associations across the lines of religion and politics and occupation, the stratified social and intellectual apartheid typical of rural Europe was impossible. The generations of young Americans were drawn together by public school, jobs, and the common bond of a democratic ethic.

In that social-cultural setting of post-Civil War America, a new approach to religion and philosophy was possible.

Felix Adler, the founder and first leader of the group which became the New York Society for Ethical Culture, was a philosopher, an intellectual, and a scholar, deeply religious in his approach to the problems of life. He was very much aware that the great religious traditions had included a concern for moral life, but for him the ethical values required no theological or metaphysical sanctions. His reverence for life included a profound sense of responsibility for safeguarding and nourishing a faith in human worth and human potential. He held that human beings would be truer to their essential natures if they faced the fact that whatever insight or wisdom they developed came out of human experience rather than from some supernatural authority.

Speaking of moral freedom and the sources of ethical judgment in one of his early addresses, Felix Adler said, "In ancient times it was believed that music, painting, sculpture, poetry were invented by the gods. Nowadays we are well aware that the arts were invented by men. We do not pretend to grasp the mystery of the artistic faculty, but this we know, that it is part of the equipment of the human. In like manner, it is still believed that morality is too good and noble a thing to have sprung from the human spirit. But we desire to strip off the garb of myth and fiction from religious history. As with art, so with morality; it too is part of the endowment of the human and one of the ways in which the human spirit expresses itself in its interpretation of experience and in its quest for a better life."

For Adler, moral freedom meant the freedom to think for oneself. In this spirit he asked himself the question, "If the Ten Commandments did not come from God through a prophet named Moses, or through other gods and other prophets, where did they come from? And if they came from humankind, what does that mean?" "Thou Shalt Not Kill" implied that the life of every human being was inviolable. But if this valuation of the human being was not divine, it had to be explained in human terms. For Dr. Adler the formulation of inviolability and worth came from the experience of individual uniqueness. Every individual was different from all others. Uniqueness meant that each was induplicable and irreplaceable.

Ethics, as interpreted by the Ethical movement, is not a set of fixed, absolute commandments or codes of morality. The issues of right and wrong are not so simple that they can be set at one time for all time or in one place for all the earth. Ethics is the attempt to nourish sensitivity, maturity of conscience and moral judgment, to foster the growth which will transcend the moral codes of the past and move human relationships toward a more secure and just, a more liberating and creative way of life.

As Felix Adler arrived at a formulation of what he believed was a flexible, progressive approach to a more ethical life, he expressed his thought in a positive directive: "So act as to evoke the best in others and thereby in yourself." He held that we should treat every human being as having worth, instrinsic value in the self. But he did not assume that he had the authority to state this as a dogma or an absolute in ethics. An ethical philosophy called for an open-ended approach which would assure human beings freedom, diversity, and creativeness. Ethical wisdom would require insight and knowledge and logic. It would reflect the growing conscience of mankind.

Although he was willing to stake his reputation and his life on the teaching that human beings should act in relationships as if every human being had worth *per se*, and although he was ready to make this proposition a central element in his approach to education, social service, and social action, he offered it not as a dogma but as a principle to be tested for its validity.

The wonder was that with all this learning and leadership in religion and philosophy and ethics, Felix Adler entitled his major work not *The Ethical Philosophy of Life*, but rather *An Ethical Philosophy of Life*. For this I am sure we all thank him. It is a lesson in humility and the expression of his belief that no one leader or group should ever think that they could achieve and impose a fixed and perfect formulation for the Ethical movement.

What are the essential functions of a philosophy of life and a commitment worthy of faith in life?

First, I believe, it should help the individual find direction in life. It should help clarify values and priorities so that a person may have motivation for learning and for developing his interests, talents, productivity, and creativeness. With such a sense of direction and purpose, a person would not be at the mercy of whims and momentary passions, of distractions and external pressures. With such a commitment he might be able to integrate constructively the many elements of his own life and that of the community.

Second, a philosophy and faith should help the individual prepare for mature relationships with family, friends, fellow workers, and citizens in mutually creative endeavors to achieve a more ethical social order.

Finally, such a philosophy and faith should prepare the individual for the limitations of the human condition and the frustrations of life. Felix Adler, on one occasion, said, ". . . we are at the mercy of nature, the earthquake, tidal wave — the famine and plague. Despite our medical science and protective and preventive efforts, every one of us has upon him the sentence of death. This we cannot, in the end, avoid. We must prepare for it. But whatever the illimitable powers outside, we have the power to change ourselves inwardly, to become beings of dignity and integrity and a certain noble courage in dealing with life and death."

Although Adler included sickness and death as realities which must be faced with "noble courage," his greatest concern was the frustrations and damage done in personal relationships. Without promises of compensation in an afterlife in another realm of being, Ethical humanism must help human beings deal with the tragedies of human existence.

For Felix Adler the concept of Revelation as interpreted by the traditional religions was unacceptable. He said, "We do not expect any revelation from without or above. There is something imminent and potential in our very natures and with sensitivity and seeking we can experience something that is beyond our comprehension in its profundity. In some moments we know a feeling of heightened aliveness and consciousness, which is difficult if not impossible to fathom. It is as if something had touched and kindled our moral nature. We know that we are fettered by many things, our heredity, education, and individual conditions and circumstances. Yet we feel the responsibility and challenge and opportunity. We know where we fail and (we know) the best in us. We know agony and blessedness."

16

Ethical Culture, as it has come to be known, was born of the creative and courageous efforts of Felix Adler and those men and women who joined to form the first Society for Ethical Culture in New York. That Ethical Culture societies were formed in many American cities — St. Louis, Chicago, Philadelphia, Milwaukee, and others — made logical the formation of the American Ethical Union in 1889, a federation of Ethical Culture societies in the United States. Similarly, the founding of the International Ethical Union, in 1893, and the First Congress of the International Humanist and Ethical Union in Amsterdam, in 1952 (with delegates from 30 nations), gives evidence of the timeliness and world-wide need for a movement based upon ethics without dogma and a humanism without sectarian or theological or metaphysical doctrines.

In its early years the Leaders of the Ethical movement were drawn from many different religious and non-religious backgrounds. The Leaders in the United States came from many sections of the country and from abroad. They were varied in educational levels, some scholarly, some from university backgrounds, and some self-educated. They were colorful and exciting in their philosophical, political, and social perspectives. They showed it in their approach to children and adults, to family life and social issues, and to the aesthetic aspects of human life. Above all, they were people who were never moralistic or pedantic. Whether they did their work in the large urban centers of the East or in the Midwest, they had an outreach into education and social service and social action which was stimulating and gave a sense that ethics was dynamic and that humanism had many dimensions. Through schools and camps, through neighborhood settlements and play schools, through original projects and coalitions on major social issues, they contributed to the growth of tens of thousands of human beings and were part of the social reform of their generations. Whatever their differences, they moved toward a more democratic nation and a more peaceful world.

In the days ahead the Ethical movement will be tested by the role it plays in national and world crises.

The movement, its reason for being and its future in human history, will be judged not by what it speaks and prints but by what it does, not only by what it has done in the past but by its role in the future. And it will be tested not by numbers of members of Ethical societies, or by budgets and meeting houses or public relations programs. It will be tested by the way it helps human beings clarify their values, by the way it contributes to ethical growth and a more sensitive and mature human conscience. It will be justified by the quality of its efforts in education and social service and by the way it helps to change social conditions and the climate and quality of human relationships.

In fulfilling this function the movement can help liberate human beings from traditional sectarian creeds and dogmas, from fixed moral codes which limit ethical growth and which have caused unjustified guilt and repression and injustice. In their insistence that only the influence of a supernatural power can bring about the good life, the traditional faiths betray the human spirit. The emergence of a movement based on a faith in human reason and judgment — and the will to take responsibility for life and the kind of society in which people can know freedom and justice — this is the justification for the existence of the Ethical movement.

We have the gift of human life, wherever it comes from, and the means of developing what is distinctively human. To destroy or waste life is to betray our humanity and to rob human society. To live like animals would be to miss the point of being human.

When we ask, "What does it mean to be human?" we find an answer in the mutual cultivation of the gifts and possibilities of human beings. For it is the potential truth and beauty and goodness within and between people and between cultures which presents our challenge and our opportunity.

In our effort to grow and cultivate eithical awareness and sensitivity in the individual, and to create a more ethical culture in our institutions and social order, we can unite no matter what our differences concerning the unknown. To rise above the laws of the jungle, of life feeding on life, and to live with others in mutually creative relations is a consecrating influence. It makes us worthy of the gift of life.

CAN A HUMANIST FAITH BE SUFFICIENT?

Edward L. Ericson

PHILOSOPHIES AND social theories are most meaningful when we meet them in the embodiment of personal lives. If I wish to understand Judaism and Jewishness I can gain a purely formal and external knowledge by consulting dictionaries of philosophy and religion. But if I enter imaginatively into the inner struggles and moral passions of a Spinoza or a Buber, so that the fire of their humanity ignites some portion of my own, they become a living, integral part of my being. The Jewish experience which was theirs becomes also a dimension of me, a portion of the universal experience of being human. When recently I read of a gang of street hoodlums who taunted a band of Orthodox Jewish mourners as they bore the body of a murdered congregant to the cemetery — the gang heckling them with cries of "Heil Hitler!" and "Hitler was right!" — a portion of me knew that I was the victim too — and also the persecuter.

To deface one human being is to mutilate something within all. Persons who do not bear this *experience* of empathy and moral solidarity are humanly dead; those who never awakened to this awareness, who may have lost even the possibility of such a sensibility, are truly stillborn. It is in this sensibility of identity — this living experience of our oneness or unity as human beings — that the germ of moral consciousness is born.

I must make my "confessional" explicit at the outset of this topic — even at the risk of putting off those who may expect a more rationalistic statement. I believe in a quite literal sense that the Spinozas and the Bubers — with the Gandhis, Darwins, Brunos, Buddhas, and Lao Tzes — are all part of our lives and our lives an extension of theirs. We must know this if we are to be truly alive to the reach of our humanity. I believe this of the many unknown men and women who have had an even larger influence in tracing out what in quiet moments we hear as the music of our inner lives — of our souls, to use an old and honored concept in a new application. Music it is, despite all the clatter and dissonance which any human existence must contain.

In a quite ineffable and yet substantive way, our lives merge into one life. We live and die in each others radiance and shadow. In our experience of others we find both our ultimate happiness and our supreme torment.

All profound religions have taught in their various guises the oneness of life, fragmented or broken as our existences may be. Many modern men and women are threatened by this overarching vision of an ultimate solidarity, considering it to be a threat to individuality and selfhood. But their anxiety rests on a misconception. Moral involvement creates our individuality and selfhood. Moral identity generates our humanity. Without it we are automatons, without value or imagination. Individuality is not born in isolation. Separatism is darkness and death; only in the community of minds that conjoin and confront do we awaken from the glacial sleep. I am not suggesting magic or the occult, but a direct moral perception — a continuum that enables our lives to penetrate and complete each other.

Because contemporary men and women understand this less clearly than our ancestors did, we are more likely to swing wildly between the extremes of a stifling but vacuous togetherness and a despairing isolation. There comes to be a clutching, grasping desperation in human relationships when there is little security in our ability to hold, or in the capacity to let go.

The remedy for this insecurity is essentially spiritual. The religious and the spiritual — stripped down to their inner core — are simply the internal forces of life that bind together, making wholeness where there is brokenness, moral intimacy and solidarity where there is estrangement. The spiritual life is thus a connective and interior humanism. In this primordial function, humanism is a unifying faith that transcends the boundaries that divide sects, classes, and parties. It also serves to heal and unify the fragmentariness and incompleteness of the self.

20

A heightened awareness of the moral and spiritual continuum that constitutes human life developed during my youth at the very moment when I was throwing off the traditional religious belief of my conservative Protestant upbringing. Even during the upheaval of a profound spiritual and philosophical crisis of belief, my childhood exposure to deep religious feeling remained a continuing source of inner security, preparing the way for the birth and maturation of a personal humanist faith.

Unlike many other children who grow up to be rationalists and freethinkers — looking back on their religious training with distaste and even trauma — mine was little short of idyllic. I accepted God quite naturally as the greater and more mysterious of my two good fathers. I admired my earthly father enormously, along with my mother. While my earthly father labored in the distribution yard of the Gulf Refining Company in Tampa, on warm summer afternoons I would look up from the screened porch of our house into the radiant cumulus clouds of a Florida sky, wherein the silver billows my "other" Father dwelled. Rocking vigorously in the green wooden chair that my Dad had built for me (to match his big rocker), I would proclaim for heaven's delectation the wonders of earth and sky — listing in meticulous detail every feature of the tall pines that stood like a Delphic chorus in the fields surrounding our house.

God was only the most regal of the presences in my large pantheon of nature and imagination. When I had sufficiently rhapsodized the deliciousness of the trees, woods and fields, with the ardor of Solomon extolling the glories of the Shulamite, I would proceed to catalogue the birds, dragonflies, flowers, and weeds, down to the green slime growing on the banks and ditches of the nearby pond. Hymnody never produced a more assiduous keeper of the inventory of all good and joyous companions of the soul — in part a compensation, no doubt, for the lack of visible playmates. (Since we lived in an isolated area, only my mother and infant brother had to endure this badly tuned soliloquy.) These childhood flights into a pure and most innocent mysticism are among my earliest and brightest memories. Their deposit is deeply imbedded within my psyche, giving emotional tone and motive power to my subsequent spiritual and moral development.

Religion to me also meant attendance in the Cradle Roll of a fundamentalist "gospel tabernacle" in Tampa where doting teachers told stories of Abraham, Peter, Jesus, Adam, and Rebecca — whom I supposed to have been contemporaries and good neighbors. Teachers gave us little cards to color, making vivid the personages and settings of the Bible. I especially liked coloring the golden halos and slanting sunbeams that conveyed the message that You-Know-Who watched benignly from the uppermost clouds.

After Sunday School even the youngest children sat in "meeting" with their parents on the hard, unpainted pine benches, wiggling feet that itched from the deep sawdust that we inevitably kicked into our shoes from the unfloored "tabernacle." We listened as the congregation sang an indefatigible torrent of thanksgiving and praise while the preacher's energetic proclamation of the faith was punctuated with the hallelujahs and amens that assured us young children that whatever was being said — and little enough was within our comprehension — was terribly important and right.

When I was seven my family moved to the small Gulf coastal town west of Tampa where my brother and I were to grow up. We were promptly enrolled in the Sunday School of the statelier and more restrained Southern Baptist Church, the faith of my mother. Since my father had become a nonpracticing Methodist — although still a believer — our parents agreed that their sons would ultimately choose their own religion, taking for granted, of course, that our choice would probably settle on one of their churches or the neighboring Presbyterians, whose educated and public-spirited minister we greatly admired. Since during adolescence I came to suspect from his guarded sermons that the Presbyterian minister was too humane and enlightened to believe in hell, I took him as my particular spiritual example, although my growing doubts about Christian doctrine soon propelled me far beyond his mild modernism — and set me free.

In the first flush of rebellion from a belief that had come to be oppressive and narrowing, I fully expected to turn my back on religion as pure deception and wishful thinking. As an antireligious stance, atheism appeared at the time to be a joyous liberation. Any suggestion of compromise with religious feeling or language suggested betrayal. Nevertheless, even as rejection of belief in the old God of Christian doctrine strengthened into a fixed resolve, I sensed within me the stirrings of a quite different spiritual evolution — the emergence of a new faith which did not require supernatural sanctions or supports — a conviction to which I could give no name and even lacked the basic vocabulary to discuss intelligibly. Nevertheless, the strong religious consciousness of my early childhood re-emerged in a new and more tenable form. Like most new converts to humanism and free thought, I was most adept in expressing what I did not believe, while the abiding convictions and perceptions that directed my life remained hidden.

Without an adequate language to communicate it, the life of the human spirit tends to lie dormant and unrealized, even by those who are shaped by its spiritual energies. For this reason I have come to believe that the essential task of a nascent humanist faith is to develop the concepts and vocabulary necessary for its realization, a language to express its feelings and positive commitments. It is not sufficient for humanists to be content in their rejections, believing that this clears the ground for building a higher civilization. If we are satisfied to accomplish only this, we may instead be bulldozing a trench in which humaneness and freedom will be buried.

For all their crimes and limitations, the historic religions of the Western world, especially Judaism and the dissenting sects of Protestantism, furnished an irresistible ethical impulse toward democracy and human dignity; it must be the task of any humanism worthy of the name to take up this moral tradition, to refine and express it in terms that make sense today. We cannot do that while we deny our indebtedness to the Judeo-Christian inheritance that underlies our civilization.

We claim quite properly that Ethical humanism is not a sect of Judaism or Christianity; we wish to break out of the sectarian mold, the spiritual exclusiveness, of the old religions. Even so, humanism is a child of their spiritual household, carrying within it the still creative ethics of a three-thousand-year-old prophetic tradition. Ethical religion appeared in various forms in both East and West, and as humanists we must recognize the universalizing elements within *all* these high religions and cultures. Light from the Buddhas and Chinese sages, as well as from the apostles and rabbis, illumines our island world grown small.

What the Aegean was to the Greeks, the global ocean has become for us — not a physical ocean only, but the flowing current of a tide of human sensibility too vast and various to comprehend except in discrete channels. Yet the business of philosophy, and particularly of the philosophy of religion, is to reduce the multiplicities and particularities of human experience to understandable and coherent forms.

As a philosophy of religion, humanism is distinctive in insisting that we begin with the immediate and the known, moving outward to the unknown, making religious experience subject to the same tests of verification that apply to more clearly observed facts and relationships. This method cannot give us infinite knowledge, but it protects us from the extravagances of runaway superstition. While it chastens and disciplines the religious imagination (properly understood), it also protects us from a closed materialism or a cramped secularism. Even such widespread beliefs as faith healing, clairvoyance, and telepathy — which the scientific mind must approach with extreme caution — can be tested by this method with the full recognition that if evidence in their favor warrants it, existing theory must be changed to account for the facts. This is not only a proper scientific procedure, but an appropriate religious attitude as well.

The oft-quoted principle of the Nineteenth-Century religion of science — "Sit down before the fact as a little child" — is experimentally sound and a counsel of true reverence. Without respect for truth, without the necessary disciplines by which we acquire and test knowledge, religion becomes a pretense, lacking the humility it universally commends. Schweitzer's simple definition of religion as "reverence for life" contains a profound and liberating realization: the attitude of reverence is fundamentally directed toward life itself and must be observant of its ethical character and basis. There is nothing spiritual or praiseworthy in superstition or close-minded certitude — whether that cocksureness is practiced by supporters of ecclesiastical orthodoxies or of secular, antireligious ideologies.

These attitudes, which provide the form and substance of my spiritual autobiography — my journey from a conventional religious upbringing to a humanist and ethical faith — had already taken fairly definite shape by the time of my graduation from high school. From time to time I tried to write down short definitions of what I believed; and when, even now, I come across some of these early efforts tucked away in a book, I find little that I would want to disown.

Most of what has happened to my religious philosophy in the three decades since my high school years has been development of concepts that were already taking form, the working out of a framework and a vocabulary to give expression to values that are easier to experience than to describe. Even when I began my career as an avowed humanist in the ministry of the Unitarian Church, in my mid-twenties, I still felt greater skill in expressing *what I did not believe* about orthodox religion than in communicating an inner implicit religion that, despite all changes in my beliefs, had remained real for me since early childhood.

When I review my early Unitarian sermons they often come across as harshly iconoclastic and rationalistic; yet even then I insisted that my humanism was religious, rather than nonreligious — believing that there is even room for mystical experience — a perception of the immediacy and wholeness of things — in a humanist worldview.

24

When I look back on those years I am aware that my parishioners often credited me with a religious sensitivity that they obviously appreciated but which they usually understood as simply a "poetic" feeling for nature. The less sympathetic saw it only as a certain facility with words — but it surely was not that. I suffered almost intolerable agony every time I sat down at my desk to prepare my next Sunday address; I dreaded the days when I had to prepare — and, quite frankly, still do — because the task of finding ways to communicate the inner life of a human being, the sense of life touching and transforming other life, is the most arduous of assignments. Describing the intellectual side of philosophy is easy; giving expression to the interior side of life is not so easy to put into sentences and concepts.

If the great mystics and poets who exceed us so extraordinarly in this awareness seem fabulous and absurd, it is because of the weakness of the language and their necessary resort to the fantastic images of mythology and the fantasia of dreams. What Melville called the "All-feeling" — which I think is essentially a moral as well as aesthetic experience — cannot really be talked about. It can only be suggested in the roundabout ways to those who are awake to their own participation in a living community greather than themselves.

How much easier it would be to abandon the effort to create a humanist faith with its own distinctive way of expressing this sentiment. How much easier to make our humanism purely a program for specific social reforms and good works. Why not just a civil liberties organization or a community-affairs lobby?

A great many humanists quickly nod approval at this suggestion — when they are healthy and the stock market is rising. But when they seek out a friend or a counselor to speak of the meaning of life at the graveside of a spouse or child, or when they are laid low with a debilitating or terminal illness and want some help in making sense of their lives, they open themselves to larger questions. In extremity we are forced to see that life has other levels and more enduring connections than our "practical" interests. Why bother with social justice, with picket parades, and civil rights demonstrations, in the first place? The answer is that they are important just because of the value we set upon human life. Social conscience and action are the essential works of any ethical faith, important because of our prior commitment to the worth and character of human life. But if we break that moral cord the whole enterprise of social justice collapses into doubt and ultimate absurdity — like a beaded toy when the string is cut. Reform movements and morally inspired revolutions have many times lapsed into savagery and self-destruction because their moral sinews were severed.

A humanist faith must have a spiritual base that makes sense, that is intellectually and morally honest, and that enables us to find a secure footing in nature and history. A purely prudential or pragmatic doctrine will not serve. The children of those without genuine moral and spiritual roots will move out into some esoteric superstition — witchcraft or astrology will do — or drop back into orthodox conformity or indifference. Some, perhaps many, will turn to political extremism or to new cults of hedonism and social terror. The working out of an adequate humanist faith, with the depth and resilience of a mature religion, therefore becomes an urgent necessity — if the ethical tradition of western humanism and democracy is to survive.

As an approach to the religious question, Ethical humanism begins with the assumption that the spiritual life is to be found in the process of moral growth. It is our increasing understanding of the nature of moral growth, and our recognition of the necessity to provide conditions enabling it to occur, that allows us to begin to express more clearly the positive function and purpose of a humanist faith.

It was this primary concern that led me to the Ethical humanist movement. It would have been possible for me to continue to hold and teach a humanist philosophy within the ministry of the Unitarian Church. Some may imagine that I became an Ethical Leader because I could enjoy greater freedom of expression as a humanist in Ethical humanism than in Unitarianism. This is not so. A slender majority of Unitarian-Universalists identify themselves as religious humanists, and I always experienced complete freedom of religious belief and expression in the liberal religious tradition of the Unitarian Church. But freedom without a clear ethical focus is not enough. What I found in the Ethical movement was not greater freedom — which Unitarians, like many other religious liberals, have in abundance — but greater attention to moral development.

The genius of Ethical humanism, its special contribution to character development, is found in Felix Adler's bold stroke in shifting the center of spiritual interest from the theological issue to the moral principle. Adler said: "Put aside theological theories and speculations as a less fundamental consideration, important as such questions may be for the individual mind; place *ethics* at the center of the religious and social consciousness; we can afford to allow diversity in our theological and metaphysical opinions if we are united in a strong moral purpose."

That ethical commitment specifies our end and the means to achieve it: respect for the worth of the person; cultivation of the moral relationships that nurture mutual growth; and unflagging adherence to the democratic process, which alone can serve the moral development of human beings.

Over and over in his addresses and writings, with various restatements to bring out the many facets of this central commitment, Adler developed the intellectual and moral foundation of the Ethical movement. There can be no question that from the creation in 1876 of the New York Society for Ethical Culture, Adler had resolved to establish the movement as a distinctive community in which the religious and educational functions were united.

It is clear from this consistent emphasis that he did not conceive the religious and the educational as separate, divisible interests. In Adler's thought the religious and educational functions overlay each other so completely that we sense his frustration at the lack of an adequate vocabulary to convey their conjunction. They are not two separate stars locked in close rotation, but a single sun.

Thus the separation of the spiritual and the educational elements in Ethical humanism must always represent something of a scandal, or at least pose an uneasy compromise. Conventional ways of organizing teaching and the spiritual life split us away from our original purpose rather than moving us toward its realization. Once we place moral development at the heart of our religious purpose, every true school becomes a temple of the human spirit, and every temple of humanism, a school.

In providing a new perspective on the character and development of the human spirit, the Ethical movement made a distinctive contribution to the democratic faith. That contribution needs restatement today, when so many despair of decency and sanity in life. Without the strong, vital nerve of moral commitment, humanism and liberalism quickly decay into philosophies of moral subjectivism and spiritual negation. Hedonism and self-pity become the prevailing attitudes, as they are already for a growing segment of the population.

It has become fashionable to belittle the liberal philosophy in favor of seemingly quicker, more authoritarian routes to social reconstruction. The twentieth century is a burial ground — and a prison yard — of such experiments.

As a living faith, Ethical humanism offers an urgently needed philosophical base and spiritual impetus to the life of democracy in our time. Those who take up and serve this creative faith are the continuators and perfecters of civilizations's most precious resource.

"SAVED" SOULS VS. THE GOOD UNIVERSE

Lester Mondale

THE BLUNT question, "Are you saved?" — put to me recently by a youthful Ozark Baptist — brought to mind vivid scenes of my own long pilgrimage of spirit. The young man and I were laboriously digging holes for the cedar posts of the new fence that was to keep his employer's cattle out of my timberland and garden. He was "moonlighting" on the job. I had congratulated him on his good fortune in having escaped the accident that took the life, only a week before, of a fellow worker in the nearby Pilot Knob iron mine. "Oh," he replied, *"he's* the lucky one, not I." He went on to explain that a few weeks earlier the victim had come back to church and had accepted the Lord Jesus Christ as his savior. So, he insited, "Are *you* saved?"

Knowing full well that this academically untutored but competent workman would never give up his religious fundamentalism for my humanism, I did my best to speak his language and meet him on the ground of our common humanity. I replied that I didn't expect to have to offer too many excuses and apologies when "I meet my Maker."

"But to be saved," he said, "you've got to accept the Lord Jesus Christ, believe in Him as your Savior."

Still talking his language, I countered: "I'm staking my eternal future on three words in the Bible: 'God is love.' If that is true, then there ought to be enough love there to include even the criminal and the unbeliever."

He was somewhat nonplussed, groping for a reply that would put me penitentially down on my knees. Soon, though, he was talking again, pushing his rationale of sin and forgiveness, and his Biblical quotations, and the necessity of belief.

Early in my pilgrimage, evangelists, invited to put on revivals in the pastorates of my Methodist minister father, did their best, similarly, to frighten me into salvation. But evangelists, as I and my saintly and insightful father discovered, have a way of playing God and eventually discrediting themselves. That comes when they awaken to the fact that it is their own platform prowess in arousing emotion, their artfulness in quickening the conscience of sinners — not supernatural workings of the Holy Ghost — that brings the sinner to the mourners' bench and saves his soul. My father's consequent liberalism — he accepted evolution and the "higher criticism" of the Bible — infected to a degree each of his six sons and his foster daughter. At least two of his children are decidedly humanistic; the others are church goers but intellectually independent.

Another milestone of my pilgrimage was Methodist Hamline University, my alma mater, with its compulsory daily chapel and its unconvincing defenses of the faith. That antagonized and drove me, for the materiel of apologetics, to Andrew D. White's monumental two-volume *A History of the Warfare of Science With Theology in Christendom.* What I gleaned from White was buttressed by the scholarly liberalism of Hamline's grand old man of philosophy, Professor Gregory Dexter Walcott. I majored under him. Then came John Dietrich, who has been described, and probably rightly so, as the "Father of American Religious Humanism." Dietrich, minister of the Unitarian Church of Minneapolis, Minnesota, preached salvation-by-science to packed auditoriums. Those were the days of the Scope's "Monkey Trial," of Dayton, Tennessee. Dietrich saw in the scientific method of thinking, and in its revolutionary product — evolution — the hope of the world. Such was his gospel: mankind taking over the evolutionary processes, shaping our own destiny, heaven here and not hereafter. I found Dietrich's services as attractive as the chapel services were the opposite.

Inspired by White, Walcott, and Dietrich, I proceeded to organize on the campus, to the horror of Minnesota Methodism, a study group that was dubbed the "Atheist Club." This included several students who went on later to distinguish themselves in education, science, and journalism. This campus heresy led to the expulsion of Walcott, who went on to the faculty of Long Island University. Devotee of the sciences, I could no longer share in the hominess of conventional religion's space-platform world. That platform was supported by four main pillars which, like the legs of the mythical Hindu elephant, went all the way down: the divine Jesus, God, revealed Bible, immortality. The platform in collapse left me in an infinitude of meaningless space and time, lost in a bottomless abyss of mystery.

John Dietrich, sensing the earnestness of my interest in things theological and philosophical, arranged for me to go on to do graduate work in those areas — a quest academic in format, but fervently personal in intent. There had to be, I was convinced, a way, other than that of conventional faith, to a sense of at-homeness in the universe.

This brings me to the appeal of Ethical humanism. It was spelled out in the life of Felix Adler. He came into my life, not personally to be sure, but by way of his writings, in my last year (1928-29) in Harvard Divinity School. His attraction was ethical — but not as champion of a commanding Kantian Categorical Imperative, glorifying duty. What caught my attention was (forgive me, friends, for my putting it so theologically!) the "saving grace" of a life such as his. In his living he illustrated the ethical more as a *way* than as command or as situational good sense. And the *way* (reminiscent of the Buddha's Eight-fold Path) led from a miserable unease of spirit to a state of psychic well-being with cosmic overtones. Thus regarded, the ethical becomes less command and more the means to an appealing goal.

To be more specific: In two years in the divinity school I had disposed of my "generals" — oral and written examinations required for graduation. The third and concluding year of required residence I could devote to puzzling out answers to my question: What did religion do for this person and that — and how? My mentor-tutor was Harvard's ex-dean, William Wallace Fenn. He strongly advised me to include Adler in my studies of religious lives, which included John Wesley, George Fox, Teresa of Avila, John Bunyan, and Cotton Mather.

Early in each one's evolution of selfhood were months, I discovered, sometimes years, of wretched alienation. Each was the "lost soul." This was ordinarily accompanied by the voices, visions, and illuminations, supposedly supernatural, of "religious experience." Interestingly, though, the lost soul never seemed to "find" itself, find "salvation," by religious experience alone. That came only when it had become involved vocationally in, was committed to, some consuming cause that had the erstwhile "lost one" working companionably, shoulder to shoulder, as it were, with and for other persons. The new focus reintegrated the personality that earlier had been miserably at odds with itself. This reintegration of self, together with the accompanying social orientation of self, spelled the "saved" soul.

Adler, in marked contrast to the others, heard no voices, had no mystic illuminations or visions, but he came out as much "saved" as any of the others of the prevailing faiths.

At twenty-five, in the first year of his ministry to his New York Ethical Society, Adler was all but overwhelmed at times with the unending procession of sorrow and frustration, sickness and pain. The problem of suffering, an inescapable fact of life, was not to be bypassed by any neat theological myth that explained it away with assurances of recompense in some future paradise. At that time he wrote: "In hours of great sorrow . . . we question the sleepless stars; they are cold and distant; the winds blow, the rivers run their course, the seasons change: they are careless of man."

His questioning of the sleepless stars puts one in mind of the plight of Robert Dean Frisbie, who went with his World War One veteran's disability pension to the island of Puka Puka in the South Seas. On the island he married a native woman, Nga, and with her had four children. Then she died. Shortly thereafter he wrote a friend: "I'm fed up with Puka Puka. I must have confused my love for Nga with love for the island. With her death it has lost every atom of its glamour. Even Mantuea Point, that I used to think a paradise, is now nothing but an uninteresting sandbank."

Frisbie and Adler remind one that the appearance of the world at any moment — the very colors and tastes and sounds of immediate surroundings — depends upon nothing so much as our relations with people. If they are unproductive, parasitical, spiteful, depressing, then neither in the skies of night nor the light of day will be found anywhere a cheering glow. However, if these relationships are of mutual respect, and are affectionate, if they include fruitful and sustained give and take in purposive enterprise toward a common goal, then the surroundings are seen as anything but bleak and glaring sandbanks. The seasons and the rivers and the winds and the stars become adornments of a heaven that lies about us.

Young Adler, depressed by the troubles of his fellow human beings, turned to that which alone can change the face of one's world: he turned to serving his colleagues and followers as best he knew how. That went on for years. Then in his book, *Religion of*

Duty, he implied belief that the universe was somehow *with* him in his efforts to raise the ethical standards of the race and ameliorate a lot of the suffering. Twenty-four years later, in 1929, an old man, venerated by his fellows, he wrote: "I bless the universe. And to be able to bless the universe in one's last moments is the supreme prize which man can wrest from life's struggles, life's experiences."

In some inexplicable manner, stars which once were icy glitters in the sky had taken on a warm glow. His Mantuea Points, no longer uninteresting sandbanks, shone with the colors of paradise. His universe had become for him a good universe.

The ethical, as exemplified in Adler's life, is basically an answer to the question of how to get from a *here*, with its possible alienation and wretchedness of spirit, to a *there*, a Promised Land of the psyche. The way is many and varied, often steep and rugged and narrow and precarious. It is no one-day, even one-week, journey. But it is no more burdensome and slavish than the hiking of the backpacker headed for the distant heights — headed for yet another glimpse of that farther horizon, that irresistible beyond — that has been preeminent among the lures of mankind since the day of the first of the Homo Sapiens.

ENCOUNTERS WITH LIVING AND DYING

Matthew Ies Spetter

MY JOURNEY to religious humanism did not originate with a genteel debate concerning philosophy or theology. Instead, it was born out of the agony of my generation.

I belong to those who, as Solzhenitsyn has put it, have lived "on the frontier between life and death"; to those who, starved and frozen, in dungeons and concentration camps, fought to live in this era which has become dulled to the obliteration of life.

We held onto our fading impulses beneath the accursed smoke of the crematoria chimneys because of our need to bear witness to the fact that the ultimately impermissible — the killing of millions upon millions of children — actually *did* take place in our generation; that a civilized Christian nation actually *did* fabricate soap from human bodies.

Ethical humanism therefore was above all for me a way to help rescue the human spirit, to struggle against relativism, abstractions, and the commonplaces of evil.

I was drawn to this faith out of a profound personal need to help restore some real meaning to such concepts as "human worth"; to help a younger generation comprehend their capacity to resist what Camus has called "the cult of efficiency."

Thus I hoped to do my share in affirming that even if faith and hope have become ambiguous to many, nevertheless a triumph over evil is still possible through our growing ability to love, which is the only deathless source of human courage.

My journey was born out of a religious instinct to nurture respect for the vulnerable, to sustain human solidarity against the devaluation of life in this most brutal of all centuries. While philosophy always fascinated me, I felt emotionally compelled to transform the notion of "reverence for life" into viable social action. Ethical religion provided a realistic pathway.

Also, I had a great need to de-mystify suffering, to evaluate it neither in the Greek way of tragic inevitability, nor in the Judeo-Christian way of "Thy will be done."

The unspeakable horrors my eyes had witnessed deeply convinced me that both suffering and evil must be settled here on earth between men and women like ourselves.

It was my privilege to have been born in the Netherlands into a family where the sense of a loving, caring community was self-evident. My father's democratic socialism was that of commitment to liberty and universality; my mother's never-ending attempt to help her family aspire to decent values was in fact a religious affirmation. Both taught me reverence for the mysteries that lie in nature and in human beings, and which must never be trampled upon or profaned. A humane concern filled our household; it nurtured me and provided a strong conviction that life can be consecrated.

Thus I wandered as a youngster from my grandfather's temple to my father's agnosticism, to the churches and cathedrals of my friends' traditions. I was encouraged to be nourished by whatever excellences could be found. This was especially reinforced by the influence of my maternal grandfather. He was a blacksmith, born in the Dutch river village of Breukelen, who had taught himself the classics. He was a most modest and lovable man, greatly honored as a mediator in his community. He taught me how to care for plants, trees, and animals. Yet he also set an example as a hardworking craftsman, swinging his hammer upon red-hot steel with powerful arms. To be in his presence, in the quiet of a Sabbath afternoon as he studied Scriptures, was an ennobling experience. He stimulated my lasting ties to the Old Testament. Evangelistic relatives urged me to explore the New Testament, but their salvationist literature held no lasting appeal.

Poetry also played an important part in that period of my life, as did the philosophy of A. D. Gordon concerning the relationship between a return to working the land and the religious life. In that connection I was also nurtured by the purity and idealism of the Dutch Palestine Pioneer groups, so much so that I felt compelled to leave my studies and urban employment to work as a farmhand. Plowing, working the earth in general, opened up a new emotional dimension. All this was deepened by my discovery of Spinoza, Freud, Albert Schweitzer, Martin Buber, and the Dutch psychoanalyst, Lietaert Peerbolte, who, much like William James, probed concepts of religious experience.

Living in the Hague in the Netherlands in the 1930s was a privilege indeed. There were magnificent museums and, above all, the libraries! Yet there was also the closeness of the North Sea, pounding at night on the seawalls; the sailing on the endless Dutch lakes; hiking; swimming; soccer.

More and more, however, the growth of facism in Europe became an all-pervasive concern. I became part of an anti-Nazi youth group and found my way into the Religious Socialist branch of the Dutch Social Democratic Movement. I started to seriously read Marx, Kautsky, Luxemburg and, under my father's influence, Paine, Jefferson, Mill, and his favorite authors, the Frenchman de Toqueville and the Dutchman Multatuli. Study, working, travelling, writing poetry, finding friends and co-learners — all this filled a rich and happy youth.

There was never any doubt during the formation of my life attitudes about where one stood. One stood with the Armenians massacred by the Turks; with the Indonesians oppressed by shortsighted colonial administrators (among them some members of my family); with social-democracy against facism and Nazism. All this followed, almost organically, from my upbringing, the private beginnings.

I was hungry for pathways to an affirmative love, to practical social accomplishment.

In 1940 the Netherlands were overwhelmed by the military machine of Nazism. I found myself involved in various aspects of the Resistance, such as gathering information for Allied Intelligence, helping to hide Jewish children and, later on, in a liaison function with sectors of the Belgian and French underground.

My family suffered greatly in those war years. Both my father Adolph and my mother Rieka were executed, as was my wife Suze. Our youngest child, Andrea, denied medical care, perished in prison. My oldest sister, Sophia, and her husband Peter, both active in the Dutch underground press, were also killed. My other three sisters — Veronica, Elisabeth, and Henriette — served valiantly in the Resistance and survived the war. Still other members of my family fell victim to German and Japanese incarceration. My father's only sister died of starvation on the infamous Burma Road; his youngest brother Eduard drowned in the Battle of the Java Sea while serving in the Dutch Navy.

In 1943, while attempting to guide a group over the Pyrenees Mountains, I was captured and condemned to death after many months of torture at the Fort du Ha prison in Bordeaux, France. Because of an outbreak of typhoid fever, I was accidently shipped to the concentration camp of Merignac and later to Drancy and Compiegne.

Much had to be pieced together when, after additional imprisonment in Auschwitz and Buchenwald, I was liberated by the U.S. First Army in April 1945. Following a brief period of recuperation, I joined the Dutch Security Service of the U.S. Army at Seine Headquarters. Later I functioned as a witness at the International War Crimes Tribunal for the United States prosecution in the case against the I.G. Farben Industrie.

I came to Ethical Culture after emigrating with my family to the United States in 1951 following the offer of a challenging professional opportunity in this country.

When that opportunity did not materialize I contacted, among many other institutions, the Ethical Culture Society in New York City. More than anything else, it was the immediate emotional and intellectual rapport with the late Leaders Dr. Henry Neumann and Dr. Horace L. Friess which became determinative in my accepting a professional life in the movement.

Problematic as I have found the Ethical Culture movement to be as an institution — e.g. the never-ending burden of organizational problems which became personal problems because of the modest size of the federated societies — it nevertheless represented the genius of its founder, Dr. Felix Adler, by providing a practical means toward achievement of religious community.

To choose a ministry in the Ethical Culture movement was indeed a choice "for better or for worse." Some of the "better" turned out to be very good indeed; much of the "worse" has been darker than I could have imagined. Now after a quarter century of this professional life, and with the sustaining aid of so many remembered companions, most of the illusions have vanished, but a solid central core of gratitude to have been so engaged has remained.

On an earlier occasion I had written:

"What matters in the end is not beautiful phrases, but whether we have helped to lessen misery. Whether we put a glimmer of hope into a child's eye . . . .

"This is what will matter in the end as we consider human solidarity as against the compromises with greed, cruelty, and destruction. We need to attain the passionate determination to make each human soul count, to be faithful to life. For in this is the meaning of the world and its solace . . . .

"Thus our living can become enriched because of our longing, and our longing deepened because of the presence of a love as yet invisible."

Life as Process

Because my professional life has involved me so often with people at the epic moments of life, I have chosen in this collection of essays to address myself to an Ethical humanist approach to death. To live intensely, without denying anything and so, hopefully, to say farewell to this life with some measure of acceptance — is that not a crucial part of the human requirement?

There is in all that lives a vital urge to continue living. A plant pushes its way upward toward the sun. Each human being clings to his last breath. This will to live is my starting point. The concern with death is, for humanists, not morbid; it is derived from our commitment to life.

Corliss Lamont has written of the way in which sleep may best symbolize the essential experience of both life and death. A child within its mother's womb hovers, in its still unconscious ways, between existence and death. Then, once we are awakened from that earliest sleep, the organisms — as it were — reverse direction. All living becomes transition from this miraculous and brief existence to finding our home again in death. All life is directed toward death.

Death is universal. But is there help for the pain of dying? The only help we have to offer when death strikes is to perpetuate what was of significance in the life of the one whom we now miss so terribly. There is no other immortality, there is no other comfort but to share, to contribute, even in the smallest way, to some integrity, some generous attempt to make life more bearable. For the rest, we are helpless before death; it is within us — it trembles within our bodies.

Between our working, trying, loving, and losing, between our striving and the ultimate silence, lies what we call life. It is a process. To be born and to die are related, each a necessity in its own way. All of it is cyclical. So our death, the running down of the life forces in age or sickness, or brought about by uncounted sudden circumstances — accidents, war, crime, natural catastrophes — which may end, irreversibly, our very brief presence.

Yet death is not sudden disaster. It is our steady companion. We are given these few years. It is a gift. And in whatever we choose to do with that gift lies our only consolation.

Life and death are indivisible. Why, then, our fear of dying? Why do we live with that burden of the concept of death as if it were a mistake, some haphazard misfortune which causes us to die? In fact we are part of even larger transitions, all of them changing and changing again, not by some decree of a Universal Parent, but by the innate laws, the processes and cycles of existence.

The Price of Life

Suffering at times of dying is often tragically increased by an inability to accept this reality of process.

I remember a woman, dying of terminal cancer, whose husband, grown children, and physicians, insisted upon the charade that she would soon be better. No one, it seemed, was willing to grant that she was reaching the ultimate transition from life to death. This denial greatly added to her suffering. When she passed away, no one could pretend that she had died in peace. On the contrary, her crucial hours of passage had been filled with pretense and insincerity.

The price of life is death. Death is not a bizarre fate crashing in upon us. Sooner or later death is a central experience in every family. Can we not learn to express fully the emotions of sorrow without pretending that the "dark rider" is unexpectedly claiming one we love?

Much of our confusion about the meaning of death may well be the result of archetypical notions of immortality imbedded in the Judeo-Christian heritage. It insists that both life and death are willed by God-the-Father. While death is looked upon as "the wages of sin," it is at the same time, paradoxically, interpreted as the potential entering upon "life eternal." It is around the remnants of such animistic mythology that the tendency to consider death and dying as "taboo" has grown.

We here in America are probably unique in that many men and women can grow into adulthood without ever having seen a person dying or dead. We are screened away from that reality by the hospitals and the practices of the funeral parlors. In the past, people were born and died at home; every family member had at least some acquaintanceship with death. Today, much of the emotional value of the physical confrontation with death is lost and, with it, a crucial aspect of maturing.

Even at a burial itself we are "protected" from seeing the body entrusted to the earth by having the grave covered with a make-believe carpet of nylon grass. Yet the twentieth-century culture as a whole has become accustomed to seeing human bodies scooped up by bulldozers into mass graves, the ultimate denial of the value of life or death. Think of what those in Maidenek or Auschwitz witnessed! Has their anguish affirmed anything about life for our generation, or was their terrible sacrifice yet further proof of how pre-totalitarian conditioning has mass civilization in its grip? Senseless dying is now entertainment. Films like *A Clockwork Orange* stir in uncounted millions the world over the silent panic that neither life nor death has much significance. That is the ultimate triumph of totalitarian evil!

The Process of Dying

On the other hand, denial of the experience of dying is responsible for other situations which I have often observed in my work. That is, that children frequently see their dying parents as already dead. This is essentially a biological, quantitative view of life, as if all there is to a human existence is the sum of our organs. Thus there is denial of the immense value of the psychological and social processes inherent in dying. By concentrating just upon the organic factors, the dying person is not only dealt with as helpless but as hopeless as well. He is drowned in platitudes and bombarded with idiotic get-well cards. As a result, a sense of worthlessness is forced upon him because his body is dying.

Humanists, agnostics, have to be particulary on their guard; if we say that we do not accept the idea of a supreme power determining life and death, we must not swing to the opposite extreme of deifying biology.

Dying and death are not only a question of science, not just a matter of laboratories and medicine. They are, above all, ultimate moments of grapsing the substance of one's private reality. Their portent is that they exist within a web of relationships that link us, one to the other, in a fabric of continuity.

From my observations and closeness to death for many years, I believe that there is often a profound realistic awareness in the dying person. Those near the dying must comprehend the immense value of that experiencing. It represents the reality of that particular life. As there is not just one meaning but many meanings to one's life, so can no one pretend to know that there can only be one meaning to dying. Dying is not just total separation but often a reaching for the comprehension that lies in beginnings as well as in endings.

Often we are too eager to pronounce such words as, "It is hopeless" or "He is as good as dead." There is a tendency to impose upon the patient a denial of insight and participation which fitfully emerges. But this is truly a shortcoming in those around him who cannot accept the meaning of his being aware of having reached that intersection of life and death. The person dying often can share in anticipatory grief which, far from arousing our discomfort, should be eagerly accepted as his statement concerning the worthiness of his life.

Refusal to recognize the importance of dying behavior imposes a terrible despair and loneliness. It prevents the ability to express giving feelings at a moment when this is more important than ever. Such denial is, in fact, a form of abandonment.

This is particularly obvious when one visits nursing homes where the simple statistics show that more than twenty-five percent of the elderly entering will die within the first six months of their residence. There is certainly a relationship between feeling abandoned — between being emotionally isolated — and the despair that triggers the sense that one has become worthless and might as well die. Without respect for life, we cannot hope to attain dignity in death.

Death, The Child, and Widowhood

Many adults, because of their own inability to deal with anxieties, still maintain that children cannot comprehend death. Again, the opportunity to share real feelings is replaced by abandonment of the child just when it needs such sharing most.

It is often maintained that the child needs to be protected from the reality of death. But the fact that a child does not have an adult's grasp of what death means does not signify that the child has no understanding at all. Children as well as adults have to carry mourning through to a private completion. Children as well as adults have to travel the hard road of learning that death is not reversible. Neither a parent nor a beloved pet can be replaced.

Can we hope to learn how to accept this confluence of existence?

Life and death can perhaps be compared with the love and affection between a man and a woman. When we discover someone to whom we open ourselves up, we do not claim that some superior power has ordained it from above. Why is the love between that man and woman meaningful? Not because it was preordained that they would meet. It is meaningful because they offer one another the comfort of appreciation, of trust, and the solace of being accepted. That is what makes that love relationship meaningful.

Life fully lived is of the same stuff. So is dying. Both are threshold experiences. Dishonesty about either leads to loss of the ability to gather oneself and to reconstruct some pathway. Think in that respect especially about widowhood. So often the loss of a partner leads to a loss of the sense of self-worth which in turn interferes with a realistic evaluation of one's own strength. At first one's friends bring food as a symbolic offering when the husband or wife has died. But such "feeding" rarely becomes the sustained emotional nourishment necessary for the woman or man who must ask suddenly, "Who am I, now that I can no longer clearly see myself only as wife or husband?" Frequently both men and women hold on tenaciously to two wedding rings, thus demonstrating that their self-definition had come basically from their bond with their partner. Inner conflict may lead to emotional disturbance when the possibility of a new partnership arises. Feeling exposed and vulnerable without one's lifelong companion easily raises doubts as to whether one can ever again be intimate with another person.

A widow once mentioned to me that she felt morally tortured because a male acquaintance had supper with her at the same table she had shared with her deceased husband. "I feel unfaithful," she said.

That emotion became more acute when she and the other man — a widower himself — deepened their emotional and sexual interest in each other. While grateful for his very presence, she was in turmoil about her ambivalences. The still unabsorbed acceptance of her husband's death led her to feel that by dying he had abandoned her.

Now she searched her mind for why this "rejection" had taken place. Of what could she have been guilty? She became obsessive about keeping her home spotless and only by being helped to realize that she was in fact engaged in postponed mourning could she slowly overcome self-deprecation. Then slowly she could see herself reclaiming her life, by building new ways of sharing and, ultimately, daring to love again without self-reproach.

But how many men and women go through widowhood without finding such transition? How much incredible loneliness results from the pressures of children or family who fail to encourage the widowed person in getting beyond the initial phase of despair and the feeling that life is over?

Death Has "No Dominion"

For better or for worse, our destiny unfolds within two sleeps: before birth and when we die. We neither live nor die unrelated, even though our dying is frequently barren of the loved ones for whom we cry out, the hands we would want to hold . . .

We owe it to each other to lessen that pain.

We owe compassion to each other and humble receptivity.

I see before me a young mother in Holland in the early years of World War II. She and her husband were deeply involved in Resistance work against the occupying German armies. Because of the danger involved in such activity, they had decided to bring their baby to friends so that it would be safe until the war's end. The child was hungry and the loving mother nursed it, holding the soft nape of the baby's neck in the palm of her hand. As she closed up her blouse and handed her child to her friend, she had too many tears in her eyes and in her throat to say anything whatsoever. And yet, what defiance of death and the forces of destruction were symbolized by the decision to make certain that their child would come to no harm. Then she and her husband took each other's hand and walked away — who knows how? — from the baby that had so long been hoped for and welcomed into the world with such love.

Yet death had "no dominion" over them. No power of affection was ever greater than the one which existed between these two young people and their child at that moment of utter separation. Determined that their child should not grow up in a world of evil, they were answering to life. Even in their helplessness in living in a country under alien oppression, they made something manifest which would outlast the enemies of life.

It was a dimension of love transfigured, of a reaching "above and beyond," to which they never gave a thought other than that the life of the child of their dreams had to be protected — even by the immense trauma of entrusting it to others — so that that larger struggle of Life against Death could continue.

OLD TRADITIONS, NEW HORIZONS:
THOUGHTS ON THE CONCEPT OF WHOLENESS

Richard Kern

I HAVE been associated with religious communities — churches, schools, Sunday School classes, and the like — for most of my life. Raised in a more or less Judeo-Christian environment, from my earliest days I absorbed a more or less Judeo-Christian way of looking at existence.

There is much about my religious heritage I have appreciated. My earliest years in a Presbyterian Sunday School class were enjoyable. I had a teacher who cared, and who also was singularly devoted to communicating a sense of values to those placed in her charge. Thus, in addition to being introduced to Abraham, Moses, David, Paul, and other heroes of the faith, I was also told of the evils of war, racism, and poverty. The highest attribute of God was love — an attribute, we were solemnly informed, all of His children ought to share with one another. I liked that, especially so because I sensed even then that love as a world commodity frequently was in short supply.

Later, as a teenager, I spent a couple of years in India and East Pakistan (now Bangladesh), where my father was employed as a construction engineer-missionary by the Churches of God in North America. Living in India and East Pakistan was a yeasty experience as far as religion was concerned. I became acquainted for the first time with committed members of non-Christian faiths — Buddhists, Parsis, Hindus, and Muslims — and was impressed as well as puzzled (Why could not they see the religious "truths" which were so obvious to me?) by the dimensions of their commitment. At the same time, I was made aware of ecumenical expressions of the Christian faith. In Darjeeling, India, I graduated from Mt. Hermon, a Methodist high school, and then enrolled at St. Joseph's University, a Roman Catholic Jesuit institution. In Darjeeling, Calcutta, and on the plains of Bengal in East Pakistan, I came to know Christians of extremely diverse social and theological backgrounds who nonetheless generally were able to live and work together, united by the centrality of Jesus to their faith. I was particularly impressed by the way in which many Christian missionaries, regardless of their theological persuasion, went about answering basic human needs — supplying food, clothing, medical attention, education — usually with little, if any, thought of theological coercion.

Over the past decade or so, people like Martin Luther King Jr., Coretta Scott King, the Berrigan brothers, Abraham Heschel, and other Jewish and Christian leaders demonstrated that their religious convictions were an important component in thier quest for social and political justice. With regard to my own involvement in anti-Vietnam War activities and open housing programs, I found many members of the Judeo-Christian tradition helpful in promoting social justice programs, and personally supportive as well.

Yet, appreciation of some of the good features associated with my religious tradition does not imply ignorance of the many problems that are and have been a part of the same tradition.

For me, such problems started early. While my Sunday School experience was pleasant enough, theological issues did have a way of disturbing whatever ethical equilibrium a Sunday School youngster is supposed to have. I can still recall being happy enough that the Hebrew people were able to leave Egypt for the Promised Land, but at the same time I felt vaguely uneasy with an unfolding drama whereby a God of love thought it necessary to kill the firstborn of Egypt, and then, when ultimately that did not work, the entire Egyptian army, to make his point. Somehow it just did not seem right. Possibly I was even more bothered by the fact that my Sunday School teacher, who, as far as I was concerned, knew just about everything there was to know, did not have a good answer to the problem either.

That was just the beginning. Other disturbing issues appeared on the horizon in due time. There was, for example, the matter of historical development of the faith.

Now, I feel fairly secure in stating that only a highly insensitive person, whatever his religious (or non-religious) background, would not be impressed by some of the heroes of the faith in Judaism and Christianity. The eighth-century Hebrew prophets — Amos, Hosea, Micah, and Isaiah of Jerusalem — strike a stirring chord in anyone who responds to an impassioned call for social justice. The prophet Amos' charge, "But let justice roll down like waters, and righteousness like an everflowing stream," are words for any generation. Whatever one thinks of Jesus of Nazareth, it is simply undeniable that he has been an influential figure in world history. The concept of love crucified is one which alternately awes and tugs at a great many people, secular as well as religious. Then there are men like St. Francis of Assisi. This winsome thirteenth-century mendicant Christian stepped in and out of history, leaving a host of admirers the world over. Only a stout-hearted Nietzschean would want to argue with the basic sentiment expressed in "Let me be an instrument of thy peace. Where there is hatred, let me sow love." The list of such luminaries could go on and on.

Still, I learned early enough in life that the history of the Judeo-Christian faith is not complete unless we also refer to other, less positive expressions. While the eight-century Hebrew prophets were admirable people indeed, it must be remembered that they were rebelling against certain cultic expressions of the faith which, at that time, did not object when the poor were bought for silver, "and the needy for a pair of sandals." Moreover, with all of the virtues of the faith associated with a Jesus or a St. Francis, Christianity must also claim responsibilities for such blood-stained events as the Crusades and the Inquisition. Within one hundred years after the death of St. Francis, the Pope of the western Catholic Church was leading the persecution of St. Francis' more literal minded followers who found the Church's (and, therefore, the Pope's) great wealth quite opposed to the teachings of Francis on poverty, and a source of scandal in general.

Whatever the good intentions, pious ignorance and misplaced priorities all too often have combined to generate the worst possible expressions of Christianity. The Russian Orthodox Church during the sixteenth and seventeenth centuries is a case in point. A split occurred in the Russian Church at that time over the matter of how the sign of the cross was to be made — with two fingers (the established Russian practice) or with three fingers (considered by the Old Believers a Greek heresy). Feelings grew intense, so intense that by the end of the seventeenth century the Archpriest Avvakum could exhort his people: "Come, Orthodox people . . . suffer tortures for the

two-finger sign of the cross .... Although I have not much understanding — I am not a learned man — yet I know that the church
which we have received from our Fathers is pure and sacred." History records that rather than make the three-finger sign of the cross,
many Old Believers not only suffered tortures but even went to their
death. Theological creeds frequently have a way of cluttering up the
mind.

Of course, we don't have to pick on the past in order to exon-
erate the present. More recently, in our own time and country,
elements in the Christian Church have been responsible for support-
ing racism, war, and other evils geared to dehumanizing man. Indeed,
Christianity has been appealed to by some to provide a rationale,
if not an ideological base, for racial and ethnic discrimination, American involvement in the Vietnam War, and opposition to domestic
social reform programs.

I suppose that an awareness of the virtues and vices of a religious
tradition, like the Judeo-Christian, can lead to many things. For me,
in terms of my own religious development, it meant the realization
of the fact that religious faith, for all the potential good it can do for
a person, can also be terribly destructive.

Religion, at base, I have come to see as a term used to describe a
dynamic process by which man moves from a sense of alienation in
life to a sense of wholeness. (It may or may not have a theological
component.) The essential principle upon which the process is
founded is an awareness and personal appropriation of the concept
of human worth. Where the thrust of the religious process is not
toward wholeness (all too often religion has been known to push
individuals into a sense of cosmic as well as personal alienation), or
where it subordinates human worth to certain principles which
diminish man (for example, a theological conviction that man is evil
by nature), I certainly question the value of that religion. There is
such a thing as bad religion. History is filled with examples.

I first became vaguely aware of Felix Adler and Ethical Culture
while attending Winebrenner Graduate School of Divinity in Findlay,
Ohio, in the mid-1950s. One of my professors at the Seminary had
studied at the University of Chicago where he had become acquainted to some extent with Eustace Haydon, long a humanist fix-
ture in the University of Chicago community and in the Ethical
movement. At this point the classic scenario would call for my becoming vitally interested in this classroom revelation of a non-
theistic, humanistic-based religion. Such was not the case. My interest in "Ethical" as an option for me was a later development.

It was during the late 1960s, while I was serving as president of Winebrenner Seminary, that I found that my "liberal" (which might be best defined as humanistic) approach to social, political, economic, as well as theological issues was increasingly bringing me into conflict with many Christians in the church and community. Such conflict was healthy, if for no other reason than it forced me to define more fully my own religious position. Eventually it became obvious to me that the concept of human worth rather than theological principle was at the root of my religious activism. Looking for a society which shared my convictions in the matter, I recalled my introduction to religious humanism in seminary. After a number of inquiries and a three-month fellowship at the New York Society, I joined the Ethical movement.

In becoming a part of the Ethical movement I have not rejected out of hand many of what I consider good features in the Judeo-Christian tradition. (When Jesus insisted that "the Sabbath was made for man and not man for the Sabbath" he was laying the foundation for a humanistic component within Christianity.) An emphasis on love, justice, and human dignity, to the extent that they appear in the tradition (or in any other religion) is always timely and appropriate.

Nor do I summarily dismiss the concept of God. While I personally find the concept more or less irrelevant as used by the vast majority of Judeo-Christians today, and do not relate at all to the "God-talk" which so often clouds the real issues (or is used simply to signify that something "religious" must be going on), I can conceive of the God idea as being meaningful, integrative, and wholeness-producing for some. Rather, I have become a part of the Ethical movement because I feel that it is a religious movement, based solidly upon the concept of human worth, which is not hampered by centuries of theologizing about things either divine or human. In its one hundred-plus years of existence, it has given proof of its ability to wrestle with critical problems and meet human needs. Certainly, as any religious movement, it has its shortcomings. Still, I am convinced that Ethical carries within it the potential to be a vitalizing force in expanding the moral horizons of man.

DOUG AND BARBARA

Arthur Dobrin

NOTHING UNSETTLED me more about professional Leadership in my early years in the movement than performing ceremonial and pastoral functions expected of an Ethical minister. During an interview for the position of Leader-in-training, the executive director of the American Ethical Union asked me how I felt about conducting wedding ceremonies. I answered confidently. Then he asked about funeral services.

My palms sweated and I felt slightly sick. In the year I had corresponded with him from Kenya, where my wife and I served as Peace Corps volunteers, he had never mentioned pastoral duties. If I had known that this was to be expected of me, I would never have applied for Leadership training.

Weddings? Funerals? What did this have to do with building a more just world? Ceremonies? I had thought Ethical Leadership was community organizing and education.

"No," I said to myself. "This is not for me."

Weddings! Would they be like mine? We had had a big wedding but didn't meet the rabbi until two days before we were married. We received a brief talk on the virtues of a Jewish home. The second and last time we saw him was that Sunday night at the altar.

48

Our wedding was planned long before we had our wedding interview. Our talk with the rabbi was formal and impersonal, like the talk with the caterer, the florist, and the musicians — a package, a commercial. We felt like interchangeable parts on an assembly line. Next week everyone would follow the identical routine. Only the wedding couple would be different.

After hours of college debates on the great issues shaping the world in the era of civil rights, Cuba, and mass protests, and after living in Africa for two years trying to develop a rural community, is this what it came to: weddings?

Something more gnawed at me. As a Leader I would visit the sick and bury the dead. Illness and death were alien to me. I came from a healthy family. Once, when I was eight, my father nearly died of peritonitis. But in two weeks he returned to work, driving his truck through Brooklyn streets. Not until my son's birth in Nairobi did I visit a hospital again.

Both my grandmothers were dead before I was born and my mother's father died when I was four. I remember him fondly: an old man wearing a Russian cap who kept a drawer full of rubber balls he found in the streets as he made his rounds delivering coal. He was healthy until shortly before his death. It seemed to me that he vanished from my life. The day of the funeral I stayed home and I never have visited the cemetery where he is buried.

When my father's father died, I remember we cried a little. But we didn't talk much about death or how much we missed grandpa. We didn't say much at all.

Death and illness were like that. Unspoken. Avoided. As if tragedy did not happen to good people.

Neither had I ever experienced the death of a pet. I grew up a city-boy and first visited a farm during my Peace Corps training in Wisconsin. Only once in my childhood did I see a dead animal. One day after school I saw a large brown horse lying on the street in front of the corner candystore, its tongue hanging loose, its eyes open and glistening, flies all around. It was frightful, awesome, and compelling.

I had been protected from this darker side of life. Now, as an Ethical minister, I could no longer avoid it. And I realized the terror this held for me.

In the nearly ten years during which I have been an Ethical clergyman, I have held the hand of a dying friend, waited hours with families in hospital rooms, buried teenagers, old people, and infants. I have had to confront my own fear of death. In the midst of grief I have been forced to recognize the finitude of life, to know and accept that I will also someday die, as will my wife, my son, and my daughter.

Contributing to this at least partial reconciliation was a return visit to Kenya last year. My family and I spent five months in a small house miles from any town, telephone, or electricity. I wrote this poem there:

Here on the equator
When the sun goes down,
Night is the master.
No one fools the night
Like people who ride trains
underground in my native city.
No fake suns try to light the sky.
Night commands respect without asking.
Death is closer by.
I feel the changes of the earth
And death has no fearful mask.
It is like the smell of eucalyptus,
The buzz of mosquitoes,
The flight of butterflies.
It is.
And I almost hold its hand.

In Kenya I saw that ceremonies can help integrate people into a larger community. For example, when a pubescent child is circumcized, the clan celebrates together to welcome the changes in life and status that the ceremony symbolizes. The ritual is both an individual experience and a communal one, unique and universal.

Weddings and funerals can be this too. Our modern society is diffuse, complex, and compartmentalized, and often ceremonies reflect this impersonality. They are banal or grossly materialistic. But they need not be.

Shortly before taking my leave of absence from the Long Island Ethical Society in order to revisit Kenya, two members told me they wanted to get married. For a variety of reasons Doug and Barbara were not ready at that point but would wait until I returned from Kenya in the autumn. While in Kenya I received a letter from the young couple. During a routine physical examination a doctor had found a mark on Doug's lung. They were waiting for further tests. A month later another letter arrived. Doug was operated on for the removal of the growth. They were eager for me to return so they could get married. We planned the ceremony for mid-October.

My wife Lyn and the children returned home with me toward the end of September and a group of Society members greeted us at the airport. Doug and Barbara were conspicuously absent. After the initial flush of excitement about being home, we were told that Doug was in the hospital again. He had been having difficulty with his eyes. The doctors thought that his cancer had spread to his brain. It was serious.

The doctors weren't sure how extensively the cancer had invaded other parts of Doug's body, but they suspected the worst. Doug and Barbara, as it turns out, had decided that they couldn't wait for my return in order to get married. They wanted to be wed before Doug went to the hospital again. So they had gone to a judge that Friday before my return to become legally husband and wife.

Doug received a series of radiation treatments but they failed to check the malignant growth. His eyes continued to bother him until he could no longer keep them open. He lost his sense of balance and needed a cane, then a walker. In a few short months he was confined to the house and finally to bed.

Several times Barbara expressed her disappointment at not having had an Ethical humanist wedding ceremony. While it was important for them to have become married, she felt something was lacking. A quick ceremony in a judge's chamber did not satisfy her, although she could not say exactly what she felt was missing. Doug too on various occasions said he wished that I had married him and Barbara. Throughout his life he had not thought much of ceremoneis but now this pressed on him. No one any longer held out hope for his recovery. One night, while I sat with him and Barbara, he asked if I would perform a wedding service for them.

Less than a week later close friends and relatives came to Doug and Barbara's home. We arranged for the ceremony to take place in the sunroom — the place where Doug's hospital bed had been set up so he could overlook the garden out back. Doug lay in his bed, only partially conscious and coherent. The others of us stood around him and Barbara sat on the bedside, holding his hand. Each brought something to say, and we shared our thoughts and feelings with Doug and Barbara. I read this poem which I had written for them:

Winter has beauty of its own:
Snow on a field
Brushing the earth soft;
A frost trellis and lace-work ice.
Home fires burn warmer.
Two cardinals in white gardens

51

Like flying rosebuds
Flower in the cold.[1]

When we were finished, Doug, who had his eyes closed through-out the ceremony, said it was now his turn to speak. And he did.

"I am enfolded in an envelope filled with warmth and love," he said.

It was as though a veil had been lifted from him, as though for those brief moments the hand of death lifted from his body and he was transformed. He spoke to us about his love for Barbara and how much we all meant to him.

"Yes. I accept Doug as my husband."

"Yes. I accept Barbara as my wife."

Surrounded by those most close to them, in the intimacy of their home, with the specter of death present and visible, they re-dedicated themselves to each other. Then Doug closed his eyes again to sleep.

Two weeks later he died at home. We arranged a memorial ser-vice for him at the Ethical Society meeting house. Whereas the wedding was nearly private, in a home with but ten guests, the memorial service was communal, the meeting house filled with friends and relatives, acquaintances and colleagues. The memorial service emphasized the inevitability of death and the loss and grief we all felt. But Doug had given something to each of us who knew him and that lives on through us. Others who were especially close to him spoke of his qualities of gentleness and humor. And members of the Society who were musicians and knew that Doug enjoyed jazz ended the service with the mellow, bittersweet Duke Ellington composition, *Mood Indigo*.

This was the closing of an exhausting, draining, yet exhilirating month — from the intense warmth of the wedding at a sickbed to the pathos of a memorial service for a man whose life ended shortly after his love began.

"We mutually needed to reaffirm our commitment," Barbara reflects now. "I felt the love of sharing with him, and the love and support of a group at the ceremony that was almost overwhelming. Without that I could probably not have had the strength to face what was inevitable. The peace and security — and pleasure! — in Doug's participation in our marriage ceremony which he requested so close to his death gives me a memory that has and will continue to

---

[1] Long Island *Naturalist,* Fall 1976.

dispel the grief and depression which overtakes me when I remember how short — but wonderful — our time was.

"The memorial service was like the closing of a transparent cover of our book. The service was really for me — to hear expressed what I felt about Doug and the comfort of others who cared and spoke so sensitively. It marked the close of a living relationship. Instead of the closing off of a dying person, I will be forever grateful for the very special way in which he is enfolded into my life.

"I can't express too strongly the importance of the *inclusion* of dying people, for them and the family, in life!"

I no longer have any doubts that ceremonies are significant. Then why are so many devoid of meaning, why am I still uneasy with many which I experience outside the Ethical movement? There are many reasons, but a few are salient. A vast number of ceremonies have been captured by business interests. They are no longer spiritual, religious, communal matters. Catering halls and funeral homes have robbed ceremonies of their power and have made them into just another commodity in our consumer culture.

Another reason why I am uncomfortable with most ceremonies is that I cannot accept the supernatural framework in which they are set. Life after death for me is only as a person's influence continues in other people. I don't believe that God is a partner in my marriage or that God blesses any marriage. I don't believe in the Law of Moses and Israel or that I am part of a chosen people.

And it appears as though most religious ceremonies are concerned with the form and ritual. They lack a personal element which touches people.

I have learned that for me to give the best that I can I must know and accept my own feelings, my own psyche. I must allow the stirrings of my own soul to reach the surface no matter how painful this may be. But I desire to be true to my own being, to never deceive myself. This is difficult and has sometimes been frightening. But I don't want to inure myself to suffering or tragedy. This is part of my confrontation:

The woman with wings
Returns in lightless corners.
I shudder in the frost
Of her eagle cries.
My hands turn blue in the cold
And my breath freezes on my beard.
I stumble in black alleys,

Struggle with fingers that ache.
I have eyes on both sides of my head.

She haunts me again,
Crying in my ears stuffed with wax,
Screaming in my mouth plugged with wax.
Her wings flap across my face.

My mad woman,
Lead me.
Take me.
Help me touch the walls,
Feel the hole,
Dance.
And fly.
Do my leaden eyes shine?
From the darkness
I can see the sun. [2]

The desire to experience the holy, the sacred, is part of human nature. Ceremonies are passionate expressions of this longing. They are acts of symbolic empathy which foster an affinity with another that forms the basis of human cooperation. Ceremonies hold up to us our vision of our highest sentiments and reaffirm our solidarity with others.

I have come to believe that it is our capacity to celebrate together and to suffer with another which lays the groundwork for our ethical principles and guides us in unselfish acts. Empathy frees us from fear for we know that others are nearby. And this freedom is needed if we are ever to achieve a humane and just world.

I believe no less in the need for social action than when I first entered the Ethical movement. But I now have great respect for communal, symbolic acts, and the power and necessity of ceremonies.

---

[2] *Bitterroot,* Summer 1975.

A DISCOVERY, NOT A CONVERSION

James F. Hornback

AS THE "unregenerate" son of a Methodist minister in northern Missouri, I cannot recall ever sharing the basic Christian beliefs of my parents and their parishioners, or even those of the modernist Bishop of Missouri, Ivan Lee Holt, always my father's bishop and first president of the World Council of Churches. Quite the contrary, I vividly recall rejecting all those beliefs — in God, immortality, the divinity of Jesus, Biblical revelation, and so forth — from my earliest childhood.

Methodist ministers and their families moved frequently in those days, often after a year or two and always after four years, in the spirit of the circuit-rider. So I can place my thoughts and feelings pretty accurately by the dates we Hornbacks moved and the towns and houses we lived in.

By the time I was four or barely five, looking at the sky from the hayloft of the carriage house behind the parsonage in Chillicothe, Missouri, I was a convinced scientific naturalist in my view of the universe, without knowing those words for it, and an Ethical humanist in my philosophy of life. To avoid shocking and alienating my parents until I could be grown and free, I practiced minimal conformities. I heard and enjoyed countless readings from the Bible, Old Testament and New, delighting at times in catching my father in the act of editing and expurgating.

I said my bedtime prayers aloud when asked to, but wished all kinds of purely natural and attainable good upon other people and all sentient beings. I even joined my father's church at eight or nine (to his amazement and pride at my precocity) one Sunday evening when there were few adults and no children at the service. For such pragmatic acts I was always deeply sorry, and I could never accept the pragmatic theory that the "truth" is what "works" — at least not in social and political relations, where lip service to the prevailing myth or folkway usually works better than a scrupulous attempt to correlate statements with the "facts" they claim to designate.

My simple yet largely secret rejection of my family's religious background and belief from earliest childhood seems rare, if not unprecedented. And my winding up in the career ministry of an organization that calls itself religious is even more astonishing, especially to me.

For me, the Ethical movement was a discovery, not a conversion, though I quite agree with Felix Adler's assertion that we must be converting ourselves constantly. The discovery of the organization came early in my first year of graduate studies at the University of Chicago. I had finished my four-year pre-journalism course at Central Methodist College in Missouri (a liberal arts college, not a seminary) with scores on the standard entrance and achievement tests which broke all records for that venerable college. (So I was told, both solemnly and confidentially.) But I was embarrassed that my final record from Central Methodist included E's (the old Missouri mark for Excellent, or A) in the required two semesters of religion, which I had postponed until my junior year on the off chance that I might transfer to a school without theological requirements for graduation.

To my surprise, the professor of religion, Edwin R. Walker, turned out to be one of the most enlightened and urbane of the many good teachers on the Central Methodist campus in those final years of the Great Depression. He insisted on giving me E's in History of Religions and Philosophy of Religion, if only to heap biblical coals of fire on my head for the vigor and forthrightness of my resistance to the "apologetics" of his advanced Protestant modernism. Pragmatism, I called it then (and still do), or the philosophy of John Dewey translated by the "naturalistic theologian," Henry Nelson Wieman, but hardly historic or doctrinal Christianity.

Bishop Holt was in his prime, and a popular speaker at the college, as was his good friend from St. Louis, Rabbi Ferdinand Isserman. I had often sat on the Bishop's lap as a small boy, choking on his cigar smoke and marvelling at his worldly wisdom. Growing up, I shared the amazement of the laity — and some of the clergy —

that Bishop Holt could admonish candidates for ordination not to smoke (a rule in the Methodist "Discipline" of that time), and not to feign belief in promises or doctrines they did not hold, and then step into the vestibule himself and light up a cigar. Some even hinted that the Bishop did not believe in the virgin birth of Jesus or the mysteries of the Trinity.

My father cared little for doctrinal questions and paid little attention to "isms" — including the theological extremes of fundamentalism and modernism. My mother was the family intellectual and by far the better preacher and teacher, musician and critic. But my father was attuned to the age of the "social gospel" before Protestant theologians took refuge in the ambiguities of existentialism to pull their faith back to "neo-orthodoxy." He was essentially a social worker and pastor, trying always to "be like Jesus." He and I were always lugging food and clothing into the most miserable of hovels, often the same places year after year. Vagrants and panhandlers of all colors were frequently embarrassed, and my mother and I occasionally reduced to tears, by his dragging them home to share our food, potluck. It was particularly hard to share when we had a pound of steak for a change, or some other rare delicacy. I objected on principle to that kind of piecemeal charity, rather than to the actual sharing, which was often warm and gratifying once the embarrassment wore off.

We were seldom hungry, at least not for long, despite our meager income. We were often invited out to dinner on Sunday, and between the Sunday service and the quarterly business meeting there was the traditional "basket dinner," featuring the favorite recipes and bounties of each household in an unplanned profusion that no one would have thought of calling "potluck."

Our credit was good, but I was taught never to use it — except in dire emergencies. Members of my father's churches, equally pressed, often chose to pay their pledges in goods and services, whatever they had the most of, whether we could use it or not. One-third went to Methodist headquarters for "benevolences" — local and foreign administration and missions. My father always saw to it that that third was paid, by check or cash, whether the two-thirds for local expenses and minister's salary came in or not. So we tended to operate as a co-op or charitable distribution agency, with a ham or quarter of beef, vegetables from our own garden or someone else's, free shoe repair or carpentry, or overstocks of merchandise. There were always too many chickens.

My four high-school years were spent in the village of Clarksville, sixty miles up the Mississippi River from St. Louis, where wealthy families kept their summer homes. The public school was small and poor, having dropped foreign language as a concession to the depression, even as Central Methodist College had dropped its classics department by the time I got there. The teachers, like those I had had in other small Missouri towns, were sincere followers of John Dewey and progressive education, "teaching students rather than subjects." Here and there, particularly in Clarksville, some knew their subjects too, and were not afraid to teach them. These were the teachers who interested me.

Religious influence in these schools was vague and ecumenical, Protestant or Christian more by social heritage than by doctrinal design. Easter bunnies and Christmas trees were quaint remnants of pagan seasonal festivals, my parents and other informed Christians were quick to point out, but they preferred to leave all specific religious instruction to individual homes and churches. Catholic families, though welcome in all neighborhoods and schools, usually went off to parochial schools in a way that seemed cultish and unfriendly to me. And the Jewish young people, to the sorrow of everybody else, seemed to be pulled out for private schools and large cities just as they were being fully accepted and loved in the mixed public-school community. I shared the regret for my black friends and playmates too (then called Negro in all polite conversation), and rebuked my parents and their generation for allowing the law for segregated black schools to stay on the books in Missouri. They responded to all these problems with a benign acceptance of cultural differences and gradualism, which I denounced then as "racism," but which is now known and revered by some of the "minority" groups themselves as the "new ethnicity."

I never saw a religiously "captive" school in Missouri, though I know they existed and may still exist, despite our court cases, in strongly ethnic neighborhoods, whether Protestant or Catholic. (The "new ethnic" Michael Novak is probably right when he boasts that most parochial schools exist for "ethnic" rather than "religious" reasons). The only captive school I ever knew directly was in Brooklyn, New York, during a year's leave from St. Louis (1966-67), when our younger son spent a year in a public elementary school which flaunted Jewish signs, symbols, and ethnic propaganda on its bulletin board, and a bronze plaque on the office door between the dining room and the faculty lounge. The plaque gave the name and role of the director of religious education of the new neighborhood temple. Our son had a good year, leading his sixth grade, and experienced no obvious discrimination beyond a few patronizing expressions of surprise at how well the boy from a black ghetto school in the Midwest was doing in the "big time" of a select neighborhood school in New York. "Minority" pupils must always feel this sense of difference. Yet I felt impelled, on principle, to show pictures and offer testimony to civil libertarian friends of Jewish background in New York who had joined me in denunciation of similar Christian excesses. They were strangely cool in this case.

But back to my own "religious" odyssey. A few of my high-school teachers knew or shared my skepticism, though they tended to clothe it in silence or in symbolic modernism — putting new or private meanings into theological terms. They were denounced as "atheists" by some students and parents. I sought out the village atheists and found them good company: a doctor, an undertaker, and the editor of the weekly *Clarksville Sentinel*. As a high-school reporter, writer, and extracurricular activist, I went to work for the *Sentinel* editor in 1935 at ten cents an hour, setting type, feeding a job press, reading proof, writing news and features, and putting the paper and occasionally the tipsy editor himself "to bed." The editor had lost his liberal Protestant faith, after starting toward the ministry, and had taken to drink and other minor vices. He warned me not to follow, but we shared ideas — including his set of H. L. Mencken's old *American Mercury* serializing Herbert Asbury's *Up From Methodism* (1926). Asbury, of the old New York *Herald* and *Tribune*, was the grandson of a Methodist minister and collateral kin and biographer of the Wesleys' own missionary Bishop, Francis Asbury, who came to America in 1771. Though I savored his writing, and chortled over the "Hatrack" chapter which told how the town whore of Farmington, Missouri, took Catholic trade to the Masonic cemetery and Protestant trade to the Knights of Columbus cemetery, I concluded that the cynical Asbury had come down, not up, from Methodism.

I did, however, identify strongly with his concept of the "unregenerate minister's son," while trying to keep my unregeneracy doctrinal rather than behavioral. The essentially natural and humanistic ethics of liberal Protestantism, or the "social gospel" of my father's day, may err slightly in the direction of the merely wholesome or the puritan, but it has no necessary relation to theology or to Christian doctrine.

So it was that I went at sixteen to Central Methodist College, under protest but on full scholarship, aiming at a career in journalism (or art or music, which did not seem practical) and looking wistfully at such schools as Harvard, Michigan, and Columbia, which were far beyond our means. Away from home, and on my own economically, I declared my independence from religion, until the fateful required

59

courses with Professor Walker. He shocked the more conservative students, including most of the thirty or forty pre-theologs out of the total of six hundred, with his rational, scientific approach to religion. He also shocked me.

Having worked successfully at the end of my second year, with many others, for the election of one of our Jewish friends, Abe Silverman, as student body president (in protest against the nominating committee's naming him one of two candidates for treasurer), I found myself, at the end of my third year, in a similar position. The nominating committee pitted me against Huston Smith, the leading campus Christian and pre-theolog, for president. Huston had moved from mystic fundamentalism toward Walker's modernism. And the same students who risked charges of anti-Semitism (erroneous, I believe) in opposing Abe Silverman could now say again that only a believing Christian should hold office at Central Methodist. I half agreed then, and do so wholly now. If a religious denomination wants to maintain its own school, that should be its privilege — so long as it does not ask for or receive tax support. A third candidate entered the race, by petition of fraternity people against us independents, and Huston Smith was elected. Some of his strongest supporters on theological grounds, and my strongest critics, have since become non-Christian and humanistic. But not Huston. As a sincere popularizer of all things "religious," he rose through the Methodist ministry, teaching, and educational television to the coveted post of professor of philosophy at Massachusetts Institute of Technology, where he openly and enthusiastically cooperated with Leary and Alpert at Harvard in their use of psychedelic drugs as ways to the "truth" beyond science.

Aiming in the opposite direction for truth and service to humanity, I had decided to go academic rather than journalistic in my English major. Psychology remained unconvincing to me as a science, and history and political science simply dull. I liked scientific theory, but had no yen for laboratory research or applied science. So Professor Walker suggested that we take my record, and his reputation at the University of Chicago, and apply for a University Fellowship for a transition from English and French to philosophy. To my amazement, I got the fellowship.

I reveled in the university courses — elementary logic, a history of seventeenth century thought, sociology of knowledge, and a seminar on Santayana. I sang in the completely ecumenical Rockefeller Chapel Choir, hearing Christians, Jews, Hindus, and humanists, including the white-haired professor of History of Religions in the Divinity School, A. Eustace Haydon. I followed Dr. Haydon to his classroom and office, as many other students did, and asked him about the Ethical Society of Chicago. His advice was negative: a good idea, long gone wrong under the ultra-conservative leadership of Dr. Horace Bridges, a brilliant and self-made British Tory whose chief supporters at that time included Sewell Avery of Montgomery Ward and General Wood of Sears, Roebuck. (They later supported Senator Joseph McCarthy.)

But the music for the choir grew so passionately Christian as we neared Easter that first year that a fellow baritone and I resigned after a theological discussion with the director, and started attending Ethical Society meetings. We first heard Dr. David Saville Muzzey, the noted American historian, speaking on Easter as "a time for pious evasion in the fasionable churches of Chicago, tempered with music and millinery." He gave the season its natural and comparative background, and we knew we were among friends. Dr. Bridges' failing health was pulling him toward retirement, but he too, for all our differences, became a friend. We joined his Society that spring. (Ironically, Dr. Haydon came out of university retirement to succeed him in 1945.)

By the fall of 1941 I was leading the youth group and teaching in the Sunday School. Another friend from the campus, Bill Hammond, a young clergyman from Missouri growing too humanistic for his previous denomination, came along with the hope of becoming an Ethical Leader. I had not thought of such a thing, but during that year we met several visiting Ethical Leaders — Algernon Black, Jerome Nathanson, and Henry Neumann — who broached the idea of my coming along too, to train as a sort of liberal clergyman at the New York Society for Ethical Culture. The quaint name amused me then, and still does.

Working summers as a dude-ranch cowboy in Wyoming and going to school, I had registered for the draft as a conscientious objector, giving purely humanistic reasons. Then came Pearl Harbor in December 1941, and America's entry into World War II. Though my new and unexpected status as an Ethical trainee was to give me draft exemption, I yielded to the necessity of fighting off Hitler and the other fascist dictators during my two years of in-service training in New York and Brooklyn. I still believe they could have been stopped earlier without war, when others built them up as buffers against communism, but I waived both conscientious objection and clergy exemption to enter the army as a combatant.

After basic training with the Field Medics at Camp Berkeley, Texas, including auxiliary weapons and qualification as a rifleman, I was assigned with a small cadre of counselors in the psychiatric

61

section of Brooke Army Medical Center in San Antonio, as it grew to five general hospitals. My two years there as a "critically needed specialist" did little to sustain my new hope in the military solution to international problems.

But it was there that I met my wife Angela, a local artist who had worked first in the Army Map Service and then responded to the call for civilians to work as arts and crafts instructors in occupational therapy. She was of old Texas-Spanish and Mexican-Indian-English background, with the improbable name of Leyton.

Each of us worried at first about the other's religious emancipation — she about me as a minister's son, and I about her as a Catholic. I soon learned that her parents had long ago left the Church, though they returned their daughters to the faith in Catholic academies and college, where they proceeded to lose it again. Angela once asked her teacher of ethics, a former Jesuit at Our Lady of the Lake College, if there might not be a religion of ethics. He answered that there was indeed such a movement — the Society for Ethical Culture in New York. The first member she met, she married.

As we continue to convert and reconvert ourselves, all of us who are religiously ethical, I believe quite simply in the two basic principles of our "creedless" creed: first, the independence, and second, the supremacy, of ethics. By the first, I would mean that the ethical life makes sense in its own terms, in terms of relatedness and mutual enhancement of values, and of those "spiritual" beings in whom such relatedness becomes self-conscious and responsible. By the second, I mean not ethics for ethics' sake, or goodness for goodness' sake, or virtue as its own reward — but rather an unswerving and unconditional commitment to finding and following those principles which seem to contribute to the greatest possible universe of value.

Beyond these shared principles of ethical faith, my personal philosophy is based on the obvious fact of values, or of valuing. Whenever a human being, or any sentient being, appreciates, prizes, enjoys, clings to, admires, or takes pleasure in any object, relation, thought, or feeling, a "value" has occurred. Values are "subjective" for most of us, by definition and common consent. In learned jargon, they are "non-cognitive" — not knowledge or sicence, but raw experience. But ethical principles are "objective," to be found and demonstrated in the weighing and choosing of values as "right" or "wrong," better or worse, for both the immediate situation and the long run.

Applied ethics has often been called an "art," in disparagement of its cognitive or scientific quality, or a "religion" in praise of its zeal or commitment. I can accept these terms if the objective, scientific quality of ethics is not denied.

To me, the strongest enemies of ethics and humane values in the modern world are not the old dogmatists, however divisive, but rather the new "emotivists" — who see ethics as nothing but an emotional assertion, whether purely personal or socially conditioned. They separate the world of science from the world of value and can give no reasons for the latter, excepting, of course, "I like it."

I most mistrust the existentialist and mystic temper in their assertions beyond or even contradictory to science. The universe is not "absurd," unstructured, or created by the viewer. Nor is it identical with anyone's immediate or mystic experience. As contrasted with the extreme subjectivism of the existentialist, or the absolute claims of mystic "knowledge," my philosophy might be called "critical realism," or perhaps "objective relativism." Things and ideas, events and relations, persons and places exist independently of their being known, but of course may be known in part.

Each of us must find his own way in the long run, despite the wide range of common experience and — I would insist — of common, external, objective reality, even in the discovery of values.

"THE SUN SHINES TODAY ALSO"

Khoren Arisian

IN THE Ethical movement, which represents for its adherents a premier liberal religious commitment, what we ultimately hold in common — despite our differences — is the view that the ethical quest is a central and enduring religious and psychologically strengthening ideal in human life, and that this quest begins ineluctably with the individual. In my own case this ideal began taking shape when I was still at a very tender age, although I of course was unaware of its formation at the time.

When I was five years old my parents, believing that some religious affiliation was desirable for the family, simply began attending the nearest Protestant church and enrolled me in its Sunday School. The church in question was Unitarian, not surprising since we lived in Dorchester, Massachusetts, a suburb of Boston, the birthplace of American Unitarianism.

My childhood experiences were eclectic. I grew up in an Armenian household in a fiercely Roman Catholic neighborhood, went to a Unitarian church on Sundays, and attended a nearby grammar school named after the great seventeenth-century Puritan divine, Cotton Mather. Later I went to high school in neighboring Roxbury where I received an astonishingly well rounded classical education — hard to imagine in most public schools these days — replete with studies in Latin, Greek, and higher mathematics. Roxbury was then a predominantly Jewish suburb in a city whose politics were dominated by the Irish but whose culture patterns had long since been established by the Brahmins of Beacon Hill, many of them Unitarian. Throughout my adolescence in the 1940s, during those innocent days when all Americans were one in their resistance to Nazism, I rode those wonderful, uncomfortable, clanging wooden trolleys in order to take violin lessons at various branches of the Boys Clubs of Boston where I came in contact with poor and lower middle-class children of various nationalities and backgrounds. Transcending all the provincial and ethnic realms through which I passed was music, a universal language for which I very early developed a bone-deep love. Music, which often stimulates abstract imagery in the mind, accorded with my particular intellectual and emotional development in every way: it helped me to define some of my own uniqueness and to experience some very deep impulses and feelings. And because of the many different overlapping worlds in which I lived from day to day, I was forever challenged — although of course I was not conscious of being challenged — by the varieties of human relationship. I could, in some rough way, sense how these varieties were affected by religious affiliation, social class, and political preference.

Little did I realize that such variegated experiences could constitute an appropriate informal schooling for my eventual involvement in a humanistic religious movement, Ethical Culture, whose central philosophic focus is moral universalism. Given the materials of my life, that's the road I chose to take, though the choosing was by no means a purely rational and conscious act.

In growing up in Boston I found all forms of ethnicity and provincialism to be at first supportive and comforting, but in the end stifling and limiting. In those days ethnicity was secure, not vicious, because it was not challenged. Roots are what we grow from; however, they are not what we are presently nourished on. It's humanly proper that we respect the truths of our past but we should not be held back by them; they should not be our present choices — not if we choose to be in a league with our own future and make our own lives.

I proved to be, as others had been for generations in Boston, a natural candidate for the rational heritage of Unitarianism. For me in particular, Unitarianism served as a wonderful leaven, a cool and clarifying contrast to the emotional turbulence of my upbringing. That coolness was materially epitomized by the church in which I grew up — it was one of those classic all-white New England Meeting-houses built on the principle of the right angle and flooded with light. There is nothing ethnic about rationalism. What I did — I see this in retrospect — was to invest a lot of my emotional energy in music and in intellectual endeavor, and therefore moved easily toward the use of reason in religion. Shortly I came to regard thinking itself as a basic passion, which is actually an old Enlightenment ideal that had become attenuated, as I was later to discover, in twentieth-century Boston Unitarianism. Moreover, in the Western tradition the rational and the moral are elements that are seen to be inextricably intertwined.

The link that unites perception and action, thinking and doing, is the sheer exercise of one's human will in conjunction with moral courage, a commodity in constant short supply. Education may help us to see this but it can't do it for us. We can be led to water, but we have to choose to drink of it. St. Augustine once aptly defined human power as the union of will with the capacity to act. Rollo May poses the problem thusly in *Love and Will:* "We inherited from our Victorian forefathers the belief that the only real problem in life was to decide rationally *what* to do — and the *will* would stand ready as the 'faculty' for making us do it. Now it is no longer a matter of deciding what to do, but of *deciding how to decide* [emphasis added]." We are back at primitive fundamentals. When the capacity for will is undeveloped, it sets the stage for feelings of powerlessness and apathy — precisely that spiritual exhaustion and moral inarticulateness that has been noted so frequently since 1945. The absence of will guarantees that indifference will emerge. The world becomes a sad place whenever we stop caring about it; since we are part of the world, indeed *are* a microcosm of it, we thereby stop caring about ourselves. It's by means of will that we actively connect to the world and find the excitement that human life can hold. One cannot expect to get the most out of life unless he believes in himself and in the possibilities of improving the world. If the individual feels good about himself but cannot identify even minimally with his society, as is the case with many today, he can only get half a loaf. A radical distinction between oneself and one's society can only impoverish the social dimensions and satisfactions of personal being.

Now most American transcendentalists in the last century had a vivid appreciation of will. They used to insist that there had not yet appeared that human being who "leaned entirely on his own character," his own powers. That is a rhetorical flourish — morally independent, self-possessed, autonomous people having lived in all ages despite the prevailing orthodoxies. The real point is that such people are never many and are seldom put forth by the culture or by an organized religion as spiritual models to be emulated. Religious liberalism, however, does consider them worthy of emulation.

This is both the strength and the weakness of religious liberalism, for in its proper refusal to universalize the particularity of anyone's experience, it is not organized around a controlling paradigmatic figure like Christ or Buddha. It's much easier to "sell" an historical personage than an idea about the kind of ideal person everyone should strive to be.

Many Ethical Culturists have been people who lean ultimately on themselves; despite their native capacities for self-reliance they have remained with the Ethical movement and regularly evince their dedication to it. Indeed, it is exactly the psychologically whole and morally integrated person — who remains open to continual growth — that gets the most out of that religiously institutionalized form of ethical idealism we call Ethical Culture. Such people are morally mature — they see their own needs, but in the light of those of others. And you can tell the ethically mature person by this sign: he never boasts that he has finally arrived; his views change and deepen as he grows; and he doesn't say the same thing in the same way this year as he did two years ago. I like to think of Ethical Culture as a movement, then, where the varieties of autonomous life may be welcomed, celebrated, enhanced, and given an honored place.

Espousal of the autonomous individual as a moral paradigm has been among the chief glories of American religious liberalism, but it has become an attenuated glory during the last few anti-rationalist decades. The popular cultural climate today does not encourage moral selfhood. Greater philosophic substance is possible, I believe, in those forms of religious liberalism whose central emphasis is on the moral life united to an educational methodology. For education assumes rationality and can serve as a mode of personal self-discovery and collective awareness.

Now every movement, has its characteristic drawbacks. A purely ethical religion, should it fall under the influence of overly judgmental people, tends to become a moralistic caricature of itself. The main defect of moralism is that it loses sight of ethics and detaches people from their humanity, making them strictly objects of criticism. Then, too, moralists tend to be almost exclusively interested in knowledge that is convertible to behavior. But since behavior constitutes much of our lives, that option is a substantial and challenging one. That thought should be related to practice, and knowledge to action, is not an original insight of Ethical Culture, but our unrelenting insistence upon it is. If concern for ethical conduct appears to be a narrow preoccupation, it appears to me that a lifetime is insufficient in which to make the most of it.

I happen to believe strongly that a cognitive ethics — the notion that it is basically possible to know what is right and wrong and to act upon it — is both necessary and desirable. We can learn to internalize moral awareness as the spiritual ballast of our being. In this regard the characteristic danger in Ethical Culture is that its members may be tempted to confuse their own tradition of the independence of ethics — the idea that moral norms are objective and not just personal tastes or expressions of society's current mores — with the moral relativism of popular culture. It's part of human frailty, I suppose, to be tempted now and then to move toward a denial of one's best and most characteristic traits and aspirations, a proclivity that surfaces whenever a diminished sense of self and direction becomes the trend. Moses recognized this deeply: every time he left his people he saw how much they were inclined to slip back into the discredited by erotically alluring satisfactions represented by worship of the golden calf. It's hard for people to defer immediate gratifications in favor of long-term ones. One recalls the argument of the great German historian, Ernst Troeltsch, who warned that an unlimited relativism can only culminate in what his older contemporary, Wilhelm Dilthey, called an "anarchy of convictions" leading to a paralysis of the will. So I must opt for cognitive and moral substance.

The tradition of the Ethical movement, in its undiluted essence, asserts that spiritual insight and wisdom is a potential possibility for everyone — which does not mean that everyone will, or wants, to achieve it, but that everyone can *work* to achieve it for himself; that such wisdom does not abstractly precede moral experience but comes with it; that moral experience is the better part of most human life; that since moral reality is a fact, moral knowledge is possible; and that such knowledge, empirically demonstrable and rationally intuited, can *in some measure* be taught and encouraged to take root. Ethical nurture, the moral conscience, is too important to be left to chance. It requires some formalized schooling. So the Ethical movement has always stressed education as a principal instrument for setting in motion the potential for the ethical striving of the individual and, derivatively, the reconstruction of society.

Religious liberalism of any species, it must be admitted, is not popularly saleable, and efforts to reduce it to a set of easy-to-repeat slogans can only demean its central integrity and depth. Eventually everything, including religion in this country, seems to be affected by the market mentality. Thus the principle that the fewer your product offends the greater will be its potential audience, is often carried over wholesale into the message of many religious organizations, including its liberal varieties. But religion is not just another product to be merchandised; indeed, the less ideologically specific religion is, the less will it take hold with strong individuals.

To continue the thread of my personal religious evolution: What I liked about Unitarianism when I first came into contact with it as a very young person was that it affirmed and accelerated my own personal growth; it made me reach ahead of myself, an exhilarating experience. By the time I was in my middle twenties, I realized I was beginning to outgrow it. I was already envisioning an unequivocally humanist alternative when I first became aware of Ethical Culture while studying religious philosophy at Oxford where I had a wonderful year of graduate studies in the mid-1950s. Eventually I came to feel confined by the lingering God-talk in Unitarianism, the watered-down Protestantism of it all. The collective pain of hymn-singing was amusingly difficult to put up with.

On the most serious level, however, I could no longer abide what had become an increasing reversal of the rational tradition in Unitarianism — namely, that because everyone has a right to an opinion on any subject, every opinion is therefore right and reserves respect and a public hearing. I have always agreed with Bertrand Russell that if fifty million people say a stupid thing, it is still a stupid thing. I would add, as well, that a wrong opinion is wrong no matter who holds or advocates it. Both approaches — that it's *who* has the votes that counts, or what matters is *who* says something rather than *what* he says — represent purely political definitions of truth. I personally have neither patience nor respect for such definitions. The moral act, of course, is to affirm the person while controverting his opinion, a distinction not always appreciated by the recipient of the criticism. Nonetheless a view that is fervently believed but is bereft of the barest rational and empirical validity simply does not deserve respectful attention. The doctrine of the worth of every individual does not entail automatic toleration of every opinion he holds. Some opinions, after all, are pernicious in effect.

Unfortunately there is in the air these days the silly idea that freedom means shooting from the hip as the impulse directs, freedom from responsibility. "Liberation" has become a veritable growth industry. But freedom in a democratic social order means liberty under laws and other norms; it is not just another name for "doing one's thing" irrespective of its effect on others.

I object to the notion of freedom as an end in itself, for it can only eventuate in intellectual emptiness, a mindless rather than a principled pluralism. Freedom has its eternal disciplines. Man is free only to the degree that he is rational and moral — this is the Western tradition in general and the Kantian one in particular. One cannot be free and irrational at the same time, and we should not sanction any such barbaric equations. In Ethical Culture we regard freedom — at least we *should* so regard it — as equally a means and an end. We have to keep generating freedom, rationally, in order to keep using it specifically to fulfill our objectives, recognizing the interplay between means and ends, and exercising our resultant responsibilities.

Rationality, in other words, is the moral texture of freedom. This conception of freedom has everything to do with our concept of the individual. Philosopher Sidney Hook once put it this way: "The very notion of moral autonomy involves a principled restraint that respects the personality of others." An understanding of the reciprocal quality of the ethical ideal enables us to criticize sloppy, illogical assumptions about human freedom even if they crop up — as they do — in our own midst: any ethics worthy of the name will always have self-application as well as application to others.

As opposed to privatistic forms of contemporary salvation that suggest you can achieve happiness, health, and prosperity if only you will repeat your special mantra every day, or accept some already revealed truth; and as opposed to those forms of religious liberalism that say you can be free by going "with the flow" and "hanging loose" — as opposed to all this, Ethical humanist religion says, comprehensively, you can be real, you can develop throughout your lifetime, but not at the basic expense of others; you might not become a general or a world leader but you can at least be yourself, not by looking for yourself but by realizing you already have a self and need but to decide to employ it with moral effectiveness — this is moral education. You have intrinsic worth, which is the real source of your freedom, not because of some divine infusion from without, but because you have, as a human endowment, moral and intellectual potential. The strongest ultimate ground of religious confidence is to have trust in one's own being: one is then ready to experience the reality of one's self.

Ethical Culture is thus devoted not to humanity in the abstract but to the humanity of the individual. The individual has no meaningful humanity apart from his relationships, yet he has no final humanity if his uniqueness is exhausted by the sum of his relationships. No one has ever been or ever will be like anyone else, nor should anyone be taken for granted — precisely because everyone is a unique end in himself; yet there are universal elements in the human condition that enable individuals to communicate across cultural, linquistic, ethnic, and political boundaries and help them to elicit their mutual distinctiveness.

In short, everyone is distinct and important, yet everyone is a social being. Everyone will do very different things with his life, and the Ethical movement can be an enriching and provocative spiritual community for those who, as Emerson once said, believe that "the sun shines today also."

FELIX ADLER AND ME

Howard B. Radest

IF OUR movement is anything beyond an accident of history and a place where some few of us still have worthwhile experiences — if it contributes to the evolution of the human race and the deposit of things we human beings value — then it is because Ethical Culture has addressed itself in direct and uncluttered fashion to certain human needs. It has tried to show how a religion can emerge without the securities of history or cosmos and around the central notion of human dignity. It has tried to illustrate — not always successfully — how that can be done within the actualities of human life, how human dignity can become a practical directive to conduct and not just a formula of allegiance. And it has tried to incorporate, quite literally, this religious insight in a universal form, building around a notion of human inclusiveness rather than around a mythic figure or a chosen community.

I have never understood those who claimed that we were "cold" and "intellectual." That is, no doubt, my own limitation. Yet, ideas, particularly our ideas, have always come embodied in the passions and actions of persons. Indeed, this movement is biographical as well as intellectual and cannot be understood if we sever one of these from the other. I am trying to say something a bit more complicated than the commonplace notion that ideas must be *had* by some thinking and feeling organism. There just are no ideas floating around out there in the universe. Even this, by the way, is sometimes forgotten in our anti-intellectualism. But, beyond it, I am concerned to stress Ethical Culture's special way of intellect.

For us, ideas aren't fully what they can become except as they blend and merge with human action and reflect commitment. For the philosophically minded, I hasten to point out that this makes us, technically, a pragmatic movement. But I think our philosophic idealism was pragmatic from the start and did not have to wait on the coming of American "naturalists" like William James and John Dewey to discover its genius.

When I say that we blend our ideas into human action and passion, I speak with what I take to be our peculiar accent. The locus and agent of human conduct is, for us, not some transpersonal force like "history" or "class," nor some transcendent source like "God" or "Cosmos." For us, human conduct arises and rests with the growing, finite, and yet ultimately inviolable being called a person. That puts Ethical Culture into a difficult position, making us unpopular in these times of corporatism. Our commitment to personalizing action and moral agency forces on us a critical stand against collectivist views. If you will, the dialectic of our movement is in its search for political realism and its insistence on moral idealism. So, when I speak of biography and intellect I am referring quite specifically to the critical position against modern history which Ethical Culture really demands of its members.

While many may say that they want responsibility and moral identity, the fact is that most of us surrender — and gratefully — to that which most agreeably removes our moral burdens. Our movement's universalism, our sense of the inclusion of all persons in "one grand moral state" (to use an early formulation of Ethical Culture's dream), always confronts this all too human fear of responsibility in ourselves and in others. This gives a special poignancy, even a tragic dimension, to Ethical Culture. It is why the words "cold" and "intellectual" do not convey to me what they seem to convey to so many others. The ideas involved in our case command our passions. The alleged "coldness," if it exists, is not a feature of our ideas at all but goes to problems of alienation which are properly the subject of another essay.

As a youngster, growing up in Brooklyn and then in Far Rockaway, New York — a premature suburbanite, as it were — I did the expected things for middle-class Jewish boys. I did well in school, went to "Hebrew" School, and chased but did not catch girls.

Naturally, our family lived — both in Brooklyn and in Far Rockaway — in a self-imposed ghetto. Christians, blacks, and Puerto Ricans were unheard of in our neighborhood, although an occasional black might appear briefly in the person of the weekly cleaning woman. Of course, the latter days of the Depression didn't lend themselves to expansive living, and the start of *the* war (for me, World War II was and is *the* war) shifted bourgeois assumptions pretty rapidly for a lot of us.

By my mid-teens, religion had become only quaint at best, and I suspected that it was actually a lot worse than that. Politics, besides, was much more interesting, although as Democrats our allegiance to Roosevelt may well have been as much religious as political. Moving leftward, I yet couldn't escape a certain cynicism toward those of my friends who seemed to me uncritically supportive of the Soviets (and a bit later, in 1948, of Henry Wallace). The Russians might be allies, but they'd been Hitler's allies too only a short while before. And besides, a beginning acquaintance with Hegel and Marx — even as a high-school senior and as a college undergraduate — told me of a kind of thinking that I just couldn't regard as liberating. So I became an early "independent," a secularist and a skeptic.

Obviously, then, I didn't start out to be a religious leader. In fact, my interests through high school had been mathematics and biology. And as I moved into my college years, I wanted to be a teacher of philosophy. But accident makes more of life than planning does. As I learned more, I became appalled at the technical trivia which had engulfed philosophy. A massive attention to grammar had replaced the grand philosophic issues of the good and the true and the beautiful. In the 1940s and '50s — here and in England — philosophy was surrendering its soul. That, at least, was how I felt. And that left me without a purpose that could be translated into the reality of life's work.

Back in 1950 and 1951, when still a graduate student at Columbia, I first heard of Ethical Culture from Joseph Blau — a member of the philosophy department and later of the Fraternity of Ethical Leaders. I had glimpses of a career in Ethical Leadership from Horace Kallen of the New School. And then Horace Friess, also of Columbia's philosophy department and a member of the board of Leaders of the New York Ethical Society, spoke with me about the possibility of a fellowship. To help in making my decision, as I recall it, Professor Friess gave me a copy of Felix Adler's *An Ethical Philosophy of Life*, which I read with some appreciation but which I understood as a skillful but dated exegesis and minor amendment of

Immanuel Kant. It included some rather strange political notions, a brief and abstract biography, and some utterly outrageous but understandably Victorian attitudes toward women, war, and the "white man's burden." Henry Neumann, an Ethical Leader in Brooklyn who I met briefly during this period of exploration, made only one point about the book and that was to stress the word *an* in the title. Dr. Neumann's effort was to assure me (and others) that the book did not represent a sacred text which had to be adhered to by all communicants. (As I reflect on this, by the way, I'm not sure but that it wasn't a disservice to me and others. In our anxiety to avoid the evils of dogmatism, we were perhaps overly anxious to deny our roots and, in consequence, tended to reject and even to derogate them. That means — does it still? — that in the early stages of my acquaintance with the movement, including my first years at the New York Society as a trainee, Adler was a very unreal and even negative figure to me.)

So in this earliest stage of awareness I was rather quickly turned away from and turned off by Adler — not so much by my own choosing but as a result of a seemingly deliberate policy. Adler was a shadowy figure, "charismatic" in a technical religious sense, i.e. touched by a spirit not of this ordinary world. Yet, philosophically, he was quite secondary and hence not really worth too much time or effort. He was the "founder," but in our kind of movement both honored and rejected for it — honored as ancestor, rejected lest the dead weight of the past hold back our obviously better-because-newer notions.

I don't know when things began to change between Dr. Adler and me but change they did, probably in the late 1950s, sometime after my initial year or two as Leader of the Ethical Society in Bergen County, New Jersey. A rather extended period of study now began, in part because I was writing a history of Ethical Culture, in part because I was confronting the daily task of building an Ethical Culture Society. Now Adler began to emerge from the Kantian shadows, although his "charisma" faded. He began to emerge, however, not as a thinker but as a master mechanic. I was fascinated with his skill, his ability to build the Ethical Schools, to organize public-action committees, to fill lecture halls. The anecdotes I heard — and which I began to collect almost lovingly, as it were — now took on a different meaning for me. They became, almost, a how-to-do-it manual for the aspiring Ethical Leader. Was it fund-raising? In nearly outrageous fashion Adler had been successful at it. Was it the problem of conflict between groups of members? The minutes of the board of trustees in New York were filled with occasions when

Adler used his "role" to bridge controversy by calling on mere members to acknowledge the wisdom and transcendence of the "religious" leader. Was it establishing a presence to the larger community? The recurring stories of involvement in the wider social issues, of public appeals to conscience, and of the fruitful use of the Ethical Platform were rich with suggestions pioneered by Adler.

Ironically, as Adler became less the charismatic figure and more the institutionalist, his ideas almost disappeared. In fact, insofar as I heard reference to them — from some few who still read him or from some new member who had, as new members will, looked up Ethical Culture in an encyclopedia and stumbled upon Adler — I tended to be somewhat apologetic and tried to turn my attention very quickly to the other Adler, the moral Macchiavellian who had nearly alone created a well-founded movement. This was the period too when I overcame my initial hostility to the neodogmatism of some naturalistic and scientific humanists and to their arrogance in what looked like a conversion of man into God. I was penetrating beneath their formulae to what I think is genuinely fruitful in humanism. It catches hold of the important idea that we are responsible for and to ourselves, and that we have only each other to rely upon. In that context, Adler's "good" ideas seemed only to echo the humanist tradition; Adler's doubtful ideas were either neo-Kantian and hence merely repetitive — how easily categories convert into excuses for ignorance — or Victorian and thus wrong.

As I completed writing a book on the history of the movement and began to hunt for a research theme in order to finish a twenty-year delayed doctorate, I began to re-read Adler in an even more thorough fashion. Of course my interest was opportunistic! I wanted a "union card," as the doctorate is disdainfully known in academic circles, and I wanted to get it quickly and with the least effort. Obviously, since I had spent years in his philosophic neighborhood, Felix Adler as a bona fide but "second-rate" philosopher seemed a natural for my research. I would be meeting the formal description of the doctoral dissertation and making an "original contribution" to scholarship by attending to a thinker whom only one or two others, like Horace Friess and Robert Guttchen (of Hofstra University), were attending to. If that sounds somewhat cynical, it is — for that cynicism is one of the deadly diseases of academics.

Unfortunately for my opportunism, Adler now captured me in a different way. To be sure, he was still charismatic, institutionally brilliant, and a humanist without knowing it (even denying it when in the 1920s signs of a modern organized humanist movement began to appear). But none of this seemed important as I began to discover

Adler as genuinely prophetic, offering the seeds of a content-filled social ethics that today shows up as still significant.

To put this in perhaps overly brief fashion, I found Adler penetrating the core issues of modern industrial society. I found him asking the right kinds of questions about it. And I found him on the threshold of useful answers to those questions. Beginning with the inviolable quality of human worth — a Kantian abstraction — and with the notion of spiritual democracy, Adler had begun to establish an empirical content for what too often had rested in a world of logically consistent but empty symbols. Adler saw in the dynamics of industrial society a twofold quality: its magnificent potentiality for moral existence, and for the horrifying destruction of that same moral existence. Today, with the demoralization of the workplace, the deterioration of vocational education into mere trade-school training, and the emergence of an industrial crisis around the problems of labor and its meaning, Adler's ideas on "vocational democracy of more than eighty years ago are still fruitful, critical, and constructive. There is in Adler's thought a fascinating and relevant social ethics that is hardly known or referred to by anyone, least of all by his own movement. And this "ethical philosophy" is far more sophisticated than one might guess from the pious references ordinarily made to Adler's Kantian reformulations of the "categorical imperative" or to the rhetoric of "worth." Adler, concerned with sharpening his Kantian notions, gave them an original content which has almost no place in our awareness but which is still original.

I am trying to make an appeal beyond the moment to some of the permanent riches of this movement which this movement scarcely knows. I am not unaware of the dangers of idolatry. I am not interested in slavish imitation nor in establishing the authority of the elders. But there is another form of imitation which takes from and departs, and which honors by criticism. We, in our anxiety to evade the destiny of other faiths which foundered on the sacralization of their founders, have missed this other, more classic, value of roots and sources to human growth.

Looking to the Ethical movement's second century, it may not be amiss to look back, also, to its beginnings. The two, after all, are not unconnected — that is what my evolving connection to Felix Adler says to me.

NINE BELIEFS

Dale H. Drews

NINE BELIEFS are central to my humanism and my allegiance to the Ethical movement.

1. Equality

One of the earliest memories of my childhood in the small Kansas town where I grew up is the memory of being taken to Sunday School at the Methodist Church and learning the song:

Jesus loves the little children,
All the children of the world,
Red and yellow, black and white,
They are precious in his sight,
Jesus loves the little children of the world.

I also remember a picture at the front of one classroom showing Jesus surrounded by children of various races and nationalities. It seemed clear where the church stood. The church believed in human equality.

It was not long before I realized that my town did not believe in equality. Black people all lived in the poorest part of town. They seemed to have jobs which paid very little money. Their schools were separate from ours. They were not served in the downtown restaurants. Many people called them "stupid, dirty, good-for nothin' niggers." I discovered there were many black Methodists, but they went to their own church. I asked my Sunday School teachers why they didn't come to our church. The teachers said, "Negroes wouldn't be comfortable here." I got the feeling that it was the whites who wouldn't be comfortable. Even the church didn't really believe in equality!

Years later, while in college, I became an active member of the Congress of Racial Equality. CORE was at that time a thoroughly integrated organization "dedicated to the elimination of all racial discrimination through interracial direct non-violent action." I participated in CORE direct-action projects and court cases in several states. I believe CORE has had an important impact in American society, but to me personally there was a special significance in what happened to some of us within the group. In the midst of a racist society, we thought, planned, and worked together for the kind of society we all wanted. Equality was more than an ideal. It was a reality in our experience together. Nobody who has truly shared that experience can ever doubt the common humanity and equality of black and white.

In recent years movements of women and old people have increased my sensitivity to inequalities based on sex and age. The struggle for women's liberation is inseparable from the struggle for an equal society. It is not enough to eliminate employment barriers and other overt forms of discrimination against women. Equality will not be achieved until boys and girls are brought up with the expectation that well-rounded people of both sexes should have a meaningful involvement in both domestic life and the career world. Serious efforts must be made to reform sexist linguistic and cultural forms, and all aspects of the sexual double-standard must be abolished. Neither these changes nor remedies to the many injustices suffered by old people and youth can be fully achieved without a basic transformation of our social and economic system.

2. Socialism

My family experienced unemployment and poverty during the depression and lived in modest blue-collor circumstances throughout the rest of my childhood. At school I met other children who lived in nicer neighborhoods, who always seemed to have lots of fancy toys and spending money. Their parents didn't seem to work any harder than mine. But then there were others who were much poorer than we. Every winter we took canned food to church to be distributed to them at Christmas. I wondered what they ate the rest of the year.

In my teens I began examining anarchism, communism, and several kinds of socialism, and in college I joined the Socialist Party. To me socialism was a belief that democracy means equal economic rights as well as equal political rights. It was a belief in a cooperative society based on the principle, "From each according to his ability; to each according to his need."

I believe the most fundamental inequality in our society is the inequality of social classes, but this is the inequality which is most consistently ignored, excused, and denied. We live in a society where abject poverty and obscene wealth co-exist. Such contrasts would be inexcusable even if they reflected differences in ability and productivity, which they do not. Sometimes individuals are born with outstanding capacities or serious deficiencies, but socially-created inequalities far overshadow inborn differences. We are part of a species which has throughout history transformed itself through work and social cooperation, but the product of our ancestors' work is not equally shared and the work which many today are forced to do does not develop the intelligence and capacities they possess. It is wrong to deny people of any social class, race, sex, or age an equal share in our common social legacy and an equal opportunity to creative participation in extending this legacy. Because of my belief in human equality, my humanism is a socialist humanism.

3. Atheism

The Methodist Church of my childhood was a conservative church, but not fundamentalist. There was more stress on heaven than on Hell, and the Bible could be believed in a general way without much worry about the details. In my teens I was taken into a "holy roller"-type fundamentalist church, which quickly discovered some deficiencies in my religious upbringing. When I questioned the consistency of some biblical stories and expressed uncertainty about some of the miracles, I was told my immortal soul was in peril and that I must pray for faith and salvation.

For more than a year I studied the scriptures, attended revival meetings, and prayed, but faith and salvation did not come. I returned to the Methodists and questioned them about God, heaven, hell, and salvation. Though they lacked the emotionalism of the fundamentalists, they claimed to hold the same beliefs. I began reading religious books and searching frantically from church to church for some version of Christianity I could believe. I searched but found no answer.

In high school I discovered science. Biology exposed me to theories of evolution, and geometry taught me a systematic logic and the need to clearly describe my basic assumptions. Now believing I must study all sides of the question, I looked into several Eastern religions and began subscribing to a freethought publication. Then I discovered in Unitarianism a religion which seemed consistent with science. At age 16 I became a Unitarian and through Unitarianism became a humanist and an atheist.

Atheism is an essential element in my humanism. Of course I am aware that some definitions of God are so broad and vague that disbelief is impossible. For example, if God is the universe or if God is humanity, the very question of belief or disbelief becomes ridiculous. A more reasonable definition, in the light of historic usage, is that God is a very powerful being, distinct in some way from the physical universe and from humanity, yet concerned about humanity.

I consider it important to reject this belief. There is no clear and direct evidence of such a being, and anything in human experience which could be explained by this belief can be given a simpler explanation. Widespread belief in God is not evidence for the existence of such a being. Such widespread belief can be explained as the result of people's vague awareness of their own unconscious mental activity, continuation of childhood dependency patterns, economic exploitation and consolation, intense socialization, and cultural tradition. On the mass level belief in God discourages self-reliance and intellectual growth, promotes intolerance and persecution, and sanctifies unjust social orders.

For me the atheist position has more validity than agnosticism. I do not claim to have absolute, final knowledge on any subject, but it is still necessary for me to make certain intellectual judgments which can serve as operating beliefs in my life. To emphasize the non-absolute character of my viewpoint and call myself an agnostic would beg the question. I also find atheism more useful as a clear, direct challenge to the harmful intellectual and social consequences of theism.

4. Universalism

I was brought up as a member of the white tribe, the Christian tribe, and the American tribe. At an early age I sensed a conflict between the tribal urge and some of the more universalist values in the Christian and American traditions, but I saw that in people's daily lives the tribal urge predominated. There was a logical consistency in my teen-age rejection of white racism, Christianity, and super-patriotism. Most white Christian Americans find it rather difficult to distinguish between these three identities, though it is no longer considered good form to openly stress the racial element in the equation. What is publicly acknowledged is belief in God and Country. Belief in whiteness is often implicit.

In high school, when I became a Unitarian, I felt I was leaving Christianity and joining a humanist religion. In fact, Unitarianism is a movement with two main tendencies, liberal protestantism and non-theistic humanism. During my twenties I became convinced that for me this combination did not offer a sufficiently clear alternative to Christian tribalism and I began seeking a place for my humanism in the Ethical movement. One of the things which appealed to me about Ethical Culture was that it was clearly neither Christian nor Jewish, but a humanist alternative not based on ethnic or tribal identity.

Tribalism is expressed in all those limited loyalties which value people of one race, religion, or nation more highly than others. Humanism is an attempt to rise above these limited loyalties and place our concern for those we have grown up with in the context of loyalty to the total human community. With Thomas Paine, the humanist says, "The world is my country, and to do good is my religion."

5. Pacifism

My pacifism was originally a scripture-based Christian pacifism. The Korean War began when I was fourteen, and I decided I could not reconcile participation in war with commandments like "Thou shalt not kill," "Love your enemies," and "Return good for evil." When at sixteen I became a humanist I had to re-evaluate this stand along with other moral positions I had taken as a Christian. After some months of reflection I decided that my pacifist values did not require the support of commandments from a superhuman being.

When I was eighteen the law still required conscientious objection to be based on religious beliefs involving a "Supreme Being." Draft counselors had told me I had virtually no chance of gaining CO status unless I answered "yes" to the Supreme Being question on the CO application form. But because of my humanist convictions I refused to answer the question, wrote a vigorous protest against the government's narrow definition of religion, and described my own beliefs as based on "love of mankind." My expectation was that I would be denied recognition and forced to go to prision rather than the army. Much to my surprise, I received a CO classification within six weeks of my application. I later served two years in civilian alternative service.

My humanist pacifism is based upon the principles of reverence for personality, loyalty to the total human community, and the appeal to reason and goodwill. Humanist pacifism is not an absolutist pacifism in that it recognizes the existence of extreme situations in which reason and goodwill are powerless and physical force seems to be the only solution. What kind of physical force is justified and whether it could ever include killing is a question of conscience for each humanist pacifist. What a humanist pacifist cannot do is hand conscience over to government, allow military judgments to replace individual moral decision, or participate in the organized mass killing of war.

Because of humanism's commitment to the improvement of life in this world, humanist pacifism is an activist pacifism. It involves not only conscientious objection, but also working for the removal of the causes of war, cultivating nonviolent techniques for dealing with conflict, and struggling for social and economic justice on a global scale.

6. Personalism

Humanist personalism is a stress on the importance of the individual person. I view it as an outgrowth of humanist pacifism. The same reverence for personality which led me to a pacifist position on war led me to a personalist approach to individual life and to social reform.

The meaning of personalism in individual life is expressed by Felix Adler's maxim: "Act so as to elicit the best in others, and thereby in yourself." In all relationships we should focus on the possibilities for mutual growth. When we come into conflict with people, they still must be treated with respect. If we show a willingness to examine our own conduct as well as theirs, and if we show respect for them even when we continue to disagree, we may foster ethical growth in both them and ourselves.

As an approach to social reform, personalism insists that social programs be evaluated in terms of their consequences for individual human beings. It opposes the demand that individual freedom be sacrificed for the collective good or that the happiness of living people be sacrificed in the name of some distant historic goal.

Personal freedom and individuality are threatened by bureaucratic mass-society trends both in capitalist and in authoritarian collectivist nations. In large industrialized societies the best hope for personalist values lies in democratic socialist ownership of basic industries and resources, a radical narrowing of income inequalities, decentralized cooperative planning of work and community life, and strong structural support of free expression, free political action, and free life-style.

7. Critique of Science

My high-school encounter with science was an exciting event. It helped me answer deep personal questions about the universe, religion, and humanity. It emancipated me from Christianity and led me to atheism and humanism. For many years I considered science one of the basic elements in my humanism.

Today I can no longer wholeheartedly identify my humanism with science. Science, which has been so effective in smashing old idols, is becoming a new idol. It enjoys widespread political and economic support. There is supposedly a "scientific" answer to every question, including questions of social policy. Science claims to offer reliable "neutral" knowledge. The neutrality is a lie. Science is an institution in the hands of established powers. Its inquiry is usually directed to questions which interest these powers, and when it recommends policies of action it obscures the values and ends toward which these policies are directed.

For these reasons the time has come for humanists to adopt a critical stance toward science and support the humanities and social studies as autonomous modes of inquiry. We will of course continue to support the systematic use of observation and reason as an alternative to tradition, dogma, and divine revelation. In this sense humanism is inseparable from science. However, we must oppose science when it attempts to reduce all human qualities to observable, quantifiable phenomena, and when it claims to offer "neutral" advice on human affairs.

8. Naturalistic Morality

As a child I had a natural impulse to seek pleasure. I enjoyed warmth and security. I liked good things to taste, smell, feel, hear, and see. I took pleasure first in my own body and then in discovering the world around me. I took pleasure in exciting new experiences, stories, songs, and games. For most of these pleasures I needed people, and being with people added to the pleasures.

In home and church and school I began to learn about morality. Some parts of the morality were congenial with my own impulses. I enjoyed sharing. I liked seeing other people happy. I did not like to see them hurt. Other parts of the morality clashed with urges in me. I was supposed to be obedient and do the same things other children in the group were doing. I was not supposed to have any curiosity about what little girls looked like. I was most emphatically not supposed to "play with myself." I did play with myself, though. Once my second-grade teacher saw me doing it and told my parents. My father told me that if I continued playing with myself I would grow up crippled and be too weak to be on the football team. I didn't believe him. But I was very careful to see that nobody was watching after that.

The morality I was taught was a negative morality, which instilled serious doubts in me about my own natural goodness. In negative morality the chief virtues are obedience, conformity, and sexual purity. All these are based on a pessimistic view of human nature rooted in the doctrine of Original Sin and in the Christian dualism of a spiritual higher self and a sensual lower self.

Naturalistic morality, by contrast, is based on a positive appreciation of basic human impulses. At the deepest level of human character is a spontaneous sensuality and individuality. If we lived in a free and equal society of plenty, these impulses could find fulfillment in a natural sociability.

Some repression of sensuality and individuality has been a necessary part of the collective human effort to overcome the adversities of nature and create the technological basis for a society of plenty. But a considerable part of the repression is that which is needed to keep people in their places in an unfree and unequal society. This unnecessary or surplus repression of sensuality and individuality has distorted them into ugly and perverse forms and prevented them from finding fulfillment in natural sociability.

Naturalistic morality affirms the goodness of sensuality, individuality, creativity, spontaneity, and play. It supports efforts to create a free, equal, and cooperative society in which all can enjoy the fruits of technology. It believes in a childhood of individuating education and sex play, an adolescence of world exploration and sexual freedom, an adulthood of relatively unspecialized work-play careers, and a variety of forms of deep but open sexual and love relationships.

9. Humanistic Religion

Why do I — an atheist — conclude my discussion of humanism with an affirmation of religion? The simplest answer is that I do so because I am a religious atheist. Atheism to me is more than rejection of a god-belief held by others; it is a positive expression of my own deep concern and experience with religion. I believe that humanity's religions are responding to something real — that there is a religious reality. I further believe that the concept of *God* is a relatively primitive and confused attempt to grasp this reality and that belief in God is an obstacle to deeper and fuller religious understanding.

I define religion as a system of beliefs, practices, and values through which a group struggles with the ultimate problems of life and attempts to create or discover a large reality within which they are resolved. Throughout history human beings have struggled to understand the world in which they find themselves; they have suffered frustration, tragedy, sickness, and death; they have been distressed by injustice and moral paradox. Some questions have been answered, some sufferings alleviated, and some injustices corrected. But ignorance, suffering, and injustice remain as ultimate, permanent, recurrent problems of human existence — problems never completely reached by day-to-day practical solutions. To be religious is to be concerned with these ultimate problems and to reach out for some larger reality within which they are resolved.

This conscious outreaching religious concern is not experienced by every individual, but virtually all human cultures have expressed it. It has taken the form of belief in spirits, mana, the sacred, Brahman, Tao, God, Providence, national destiny, utopia, etc. Which one of these beliefs is held by any particular group is dependent on many factors in the group's life, including its way of obtaining material life needs, its technological level, its cultural tradition, its kinship and child-rearing patterns, its form of government, and its class system.

The existence of a larger reality is confirmed in the experience of many individuals. There is in them an awareness, sometimes dim and sometimes clear, of something beyond their individual rational consciousness. At times they experience a special presence, a source of strength and understanding greater than they normally possess. These may be times of joy or sorrow. They may occur in church or in the street. They may come as the result of disciplined meditation or with unexpected spontaneity.

These experiences with a larger reality are based on the fact that we forget and repress some of the most important experiences of our lives, particularly the early social experiences which formed our individuality. This creates in each of us a vast reservoir of potential religious experience, though people rarely understand that it is their own creation. Instead of realizing that the strength, inspiration, and understanding they experience is human in origin, they project these qualities onto the God they have created and imagine they can acquire these qualities only by obeying God or those who speak for Him.

My humanistic religion is an atheist religion because it emphatically denies that the larger reality is something outside of humanity. Humanity itself is the larger reality, a reality experienced in a sense of kinship with humanity as a whole, a responsiveness to the humanity in those whom we meet, and a vision of humanity as it yet may be.

NO ONE OF US IS ENTIRELY STRONG ALONE

George E. Beauchamp

EVERY AGE has had its pious hypocrisies, but they surely crested during the Victorian Age, roughly the century that culminated in World War I. The American people particularly were engulfed by the still-familiar assurances: "Be good and you'll be happy," "True merit is always rewarded," "God tempers the wind to the shorn lamb," "Blessed are the poor." (The actual Bible verse is, "Blessed are the poor in spirit," which is a somewhat different thing). Also: "Hard work never hurt anybody," "Every child has the chance to be President," "This is the land of opportunity, with liberty and justice for all," and "It *pays* to be honest."

The fact that any intelligent person could see from his own experience and that of those around him that these assertions and a multitude of other moral precepts were untrue, or simply irrelevant to the realities of his life, created deepening skepticism. The First World War did not sweep away the fraudulent phrases. They surrounded me during my boyhood in the 1920s, and we have plenty of them with us yet. But World War I did explode the simple acceptance of them, and ushered in a period of increasing questioning of all the old verities, until by now no moral standard, no concepts of good and evil, no ethical formulation stands unchallenged. Each must prove its case anew within an audience often predisposed to disbelief.

Some at all levels of life have, frankly or not, abandoned all moral laws except those of expedience and presumed self-advantage. The results range all the way from our own street corners to the halls of government, and to a maelstrom of international insanity. Others of our well-intentioned citizens share the viewpoint of a friend of mine who said to me, "Frankly, I don't know what's right and wrong anymore, and I don't bother my head about it. I try to do the things that seem commonly accepted, and avoid things the community seems to frown on. I try to keep out of jail and off relief, and for the rest of it, I just drift along and hope I'll come out all right." A jellyfish or a lemming could not express it better.

Progress from Jellyfish to Homo Sapiens

My own early experience was not too different. Growing up in small Indiana towns, I accepted with little question the moral standards of those around me, and I mouthed without thinking much about them the pious phrases and the well-worn adages and maxims of the era. I happened to be born into a Methodist home, and for twenty-four years of my life I went to a Methodist church and Sunday School without undue concern that no place along the way was I given any clear idea of what such a commitment meant or involved.

I was not without curiousity about other religious faiths, but among my friends and acquaintances I found no answers. The local Carnegie Library had not a single book in the field of comparative religion, nor, surprisingly, did the denominational college to whose library I had access. Among its more than 100,000 volumes were whole shelves of pious exhortations about various phases of protestant Christianity, but not a single book about Judaism, let alone Mohammadanism, Hinduism, Buddhism, or any of the other faiths to which fellow inhabitants of our planet have given their allegiance. True, I learned of the religions of Greece and Rome in mythology courses, but always with the strength and philosophical depth of them dissolved into namby-pamby childishness.

I had heard somewhere of Robert G. Ingersoll, and went searching for *Some Mistakes of Moses* — unavailable except through the state library — but was firmly discouraged. "It would only unsettle your faith," I was told, "to read the works of a wicked atheist."

It was not until I was in graduate school, and in connection with one of my research projects had to study the life of John Wesley and the development of Methodism, that I suddenly discovered that whatever else I believed, it was not in salvation by faith and the emotional experience of grace which should drive out all desire for earthly pleasures. And with a great wakening light, I realized that whatever else I had been, I had never been a Methodist.

Fortunately, by this time a wealth of books on philosophy and comparative religions had become available to me while I did advance research in Northwestern and Harvard University libraries. Plato and Aristotle, Emerson and William James, Dewey and Bertrand Russell formed my introduction to philosophy, and my inquiry into comparative religions started with Mormonism, the Ramayana, and literature of the Sikhs and Jains. They were fascinating windows to a new world, and I found many scattered ideas to which I could give assent, but no approach that was satisfyingly complete.

It would be pleasant to say that at this point I discovered Ethical Culture. Alas, I had never heard of it. Instead, I continued on an intermittent search among the religious groups and philosophical outlooks that were available around me. At least I did begin to question what I really believed and did not believe, and to reject some of the easy shiboleths and comfortable aphorisms with which I had been surrounded.

Mine was not a traumatic rejection or conversion. When my neighbor and dear friend Leo Wolfsohn discovered that there was a war-time group of displaced Ethical Culturists in Washington, D.C., and carried me with him to a meeting, my immediate delighted reaction was, "Where has this wonderful thing been all my life?" At succeeding meetings I listened to Al Black and Henry Neumann and David Saville Muzzey and Jerry Nathanson, and I read all the books and pamphlets they or others could suggest to me.

What entranced me? First of all, the realization that here was a group that *required*, rather than inhibited, complete honesty in the search for what each of us most deeply believed. We did not necessarily agree with each other on the answers we reached, for no article of belief was required. A compelled belief is not a true belief. Instead, we shared in the ethical questions we asked, and in a sense of their importance.

The Basic Ethical Questions

Then and now, the most basic of those questions seem to me to fall into three broad categories. First is the relationship of man with the universe, the infinite. To appreciate and feel at one with, and at home within, an immensity of time and space so incomprehensible is a quest for which different beings find a multitude of answers. One man finds a link between finite and infinite and calls it

God and a state of grace. Another finds comfort in the indestructibility of matter and the persistence of spirit. Others find satisfaction in what they perceive of natural law and harmony in the universe, and still others find peace in contemplating natural beauty, both animate and inanimate, in the world about them of which they are a part. There is neither need nor possibility that all human beings should follow the same path, but each one must find his own answer, or be alienated and alone amidst the immensity.

Second is the relationship of a human being with himself. Who am I? What do I really want from this brief life of mine, this taste that I have of the experience of living? And if and when I have achieved my desire, what then? With Omar Khayyam I face the fact that "The worldly hope men set their hearts upon Turns ashes or it prospers, And anon . . . . " The ambitions that drive us, for wealth or fame or status, even should we achieve them, will they give us satisfaction? Too many of us spend our precious days in a frenzied drive after illusions of satisfaction, down deadend bypaths that mire us far from what we really want out of life. The religious quest, in my definition, is for a longer and clearer vision of our goals. No life is free from error, but the considered life will make fewer and less costly ones.

An ultimate goal of every human being is significance. How can I achieve it? Not in the ultimate scheme of things, where the most that anyone can leave across the eons is an anonymous impact, but in the significance that I myself can find from my own experience of living. Some of us find it in the love that we can feel, and that we inspire in those around us. Some of us find it in the growth and hope and opportunities that we can bring into others' lives. Some of us find it in the strength that we can summon to stand firm for our deeply held beliefs, and for our own ultimate dignity as human beings, facing our fate, even though it be unknown to any other human being, serene in the consciousness that in the testing we stood firm. But perhaps we did not stand firm. We, each of us, sometimes stumble and fall. No one of us is ever the person we would wish ourselves to be. Our satisfaction must be that after every collapse we rose again and struggled forward with whatever strength was in us. Ultimately it is the worthiness of our goal that counts, rather than our achievement of it.

Sadly, this matter of "significance" is not just a matter of living with ourselves, of coming to terms with ourselves. Many succeed in doing that, on the tawdriest and most ignoble of levels. The question, rather, is with what sort of self ought I to want to live. Not what I was, but what I sought to be, is the ultimate measure of my significance.

The third broad area is in our relationship with others. Here the range of answers will be even more varied than for the other two. Our children, our loved ones, the development and the improvement of our own community, the prevention of injustice, a more equitable social order, freedom from the scourges of war and sickness, ultimately an opportunity for every human being to develop his potentialities, without the shackles of hunger, ignorance or oppression — these begin to suggest the range of our proper concerns. Each of us, if we are to find ultimate significance in ourselves, must transcend the encapsulated boundaries of self and spend himself for others. Each of us is unique, unduplicated, and unduplicable in all the countless other lives that share our universe today, or have shared it, or will share it. But our only sure immortality lies in the extent to which we can sense in all those other personalities the hopes, the desires, the needs, and the aspirations which we all share, have shared, will share, as human beings, and can say with understanding, in a paraphrase of Jesus' famous line, "Inasmuch as I have done it for the least of these, my brethren, I have done it unto me."

Our Common Ground

Our individual search for truth obligates us to the acceptance and use of the best thought and knowledge available to us, whether it be in psychology, physiology, sociology, political science, or all the fields of expanding knowledge that have pertinence to the human condition. Our individual differences arise not as to these obligations, but in the varying degrees of our knowledge and understanding, our sense of relative priorities, and our judgments as to the best techniques and means for reaching our ethical goals. We must learn to live with what we see as others' imperfections, not rejecting even when we cannot make them see our truths. None of us is fully ethical; we are fallible human beings who are striving together to be more nearly ethical.

Together is the key word. No one of us is entirely strong alone. Each of us has his moments of weakness, uncertainty, discouragement, and confusion. We need the support and companionship of others who share with us in our search, and bear with us even when our answers are not the same. We need a sounding board for our own attempted conclusions, and the challenge to new concepts and new viewpoints which our ethically seeking fellows can provide.

BEYOND ATHEISM: FROM J. C. PENNEY
TO THE GOOD OF THE MANY

Donald D. Montagna

MY INTEREST in ethics was quietly born in the bosom of my early family life. By my fourth birthday my parents had departed their immigrant Italian communities and settled in an Irish-Catholic neighborhood. Catholicism was our common ground. My parents took their responsibilities seriously and lived by the Law of God and His Church. Each Monday after school my brother and I were sent to cathechism class, and we were encouraged, but not forced, to say evening and morning prayers. Our family attended Mass together each Sunday and Holy Day of Obligation. My parents said a daily rosary for many years.

As a child I was sincerely interested in my religion. My natural curiosity sought answers: Where did I come from? What would become of me? How should I live my life? The Church made it clear that "goodness" was the ideal behavior. Not only was goodness achieved by learning about it, but also by being an obedient student (in this way one could win appreciation from the priest and parents while avoiding punishment from the nun).

Contradictions, however, soon became obvious. The same act which one authority approved would elicit disapproval from another. What value is goodness as an ideal if its indicator — approval — is relative? This dilemma was neatly resolved by postulating an omniscient Authority who knew exactly how one should behave and had the power to dispense approval throughout one's life and beyond. Thus, Catholicism provided a form of early emotional security.

The seeds of my dissatisfaction sprouted again, though. God's grace and good fortune are quite mysterious. It was difficult to use divine approval to validate the appropriateness of my behavior. Without objective premises, "being good" easily became "being pleasing to adults." Although it purported to be the one true way of life, the Church offered me little practical guidance or insight into the question of behavior. No matter how fervently I prayed, no matter how faithfully I kept the sacraments, I remained confused about the nature of life itself. I could recite nearly one thousand commandments and aphorisms, but I could not apply them to my daily life. As I learned more about the secular world and other religions, Catholicism began to seem arbitrary, a pomp without real-world significance. As I sought my own identity, I needed clearer answers, but the Church did not encourage me to seek greater insight into Catholic theology.

Everyday Catholicism can easily degenerate into idolatry and superstitious ritual in which good spirits are beseeched to overcome evil ones. When the focal point of religion appears to be the community, ritual, imagery, and theology, it is easy to forget that life is an individual journey. We are responsible for ourselves whether we consciously accept that responsibility or not. Religion must teach responsibility, for the greatest sin is not displeasing authority but deceiving oneself. Christian fundamentalists encourage one another to become "reborn" by accepting Jesus as a personal savior — that is, to take responsibility for one's own behavior and for the well-being of all humanity as Jesus did. Among Catholics the locus of responsibility is kept within the priesthood, thereby diminishing faith in the individual's ability to pursue his or her own religious path. In addition, the theological assumption that our animal nature is prone to evil promotes the notion that human beings are fundamentally untrustworthy. My curiosity about life would not be contained by my Catholicism.

My childhood impression of religious experience was the pageantry common in Catholic worship. However, the repetition of intricate rituals did not deepen my religious experience. I became bored because I was too aware of the ritual itself and too ignorant of the subject of worship. I worshiped the vague images of a knowing, powerful daddy, a loving obedient son, and a pure daughter/mother. But gods are no more than symbols to embody the qualities which humans have discovered to be ultimate ideals: total knowledge, love, and power. Ideally, religions are human instruments designed to provide people a way to increase their capacity for knowledge, experience, and power. Not the kind of technological learning we get from schools or factories or offices, but an awareness about life that transcends all other kinds of knowledge we possess. To "move closer to God" or to "become one with God" is to expand one's consciousness of reality.

These religious experiences, whether they are called such or not, are common to all people. They are the emergent experiences wherein we are forever altered by loss of an ignorance. They are more prevalent in those who consciously seek them. Church laws are ideally no more than guidelines designed to provide a path toward such awakenings. If one confuses organizational ritual with religious experience, then one deprives oneself of greater knowledge, experience, and power. Certainly the self-deception would be the same whether the ritual includes swallowing the Body and Blood at the altar or chewing clever intellectualisms at the Ethical Society. And church had not conveyed to me any distinction between church ritual and religious experience.

In middle adolescence I rejected Catholicism and theism as well, but I have discovered that many of my current assumptions about reality were inherent in my early experience of Catholicism. It was the Church which first affirmed for me that life had meaning, that there was more than chaos, that order was indeed preferable. The image of God the Creator gave unity to the universe, kinship and commonality to humanity, and individual worth to each human being. Catholicism taught that some behaviors are sins, literally mistakes, which need to be acknowledged. Finally, my first experience of belonging to a community larger than my family came from my participation in the Church. For these gifts I am indebted.

Another major influence upon my emerging values was my academic education. At church I memorized and believed. At public school I was told never to believe but to find out for myself. Science and knowledge represented power. They were the power to conquer nature, produce great wealth, prolong life, win wars. In the classroom pragmatic achievement was the highest value. Teachers cajoled and manipulated students to behave and learn, while students pleased the teacher for good grades and competed with each other for superiority. Here was the practical understanding of life which had eluded me in Catholicism. Life could be observed objectively, judged rationally, lived so as to maximize achievement.

It was only another short step to assume that success was the ultimate measure of one's worth. As I investigated alternative careers, the business world appeared to offer the most attractive summits. Wealth seemed the very fuel of life and civilization. Therefore, producing wealth must be the noblest as well as the most lucrative profession. Business is pragmatic, not cluttered with superfluous values. Effective ideas, properly implemented, result in success which is measured by profit. Behavior is kept within cooperative limits by competing self-interest with no pious and arbitrary restraints needed. I confidently entered the adult world an atheist, nihilist, rationalist, and a man of business.

I chose New York because it was the biggest city in America, and I sought the stimulation of unlimited opportunity. I rapidly advanced from a merchandising trainee with the J. C. Penney national buying office to an assistant buyer responsible for supplying women's coordinated sportswear to 1800 stores. To be courted by winsome fashion designers, wily wheeler-dealers, and the messengers of venerated garment barons can be very intoxicating to a young man from Massachusetts. The pace was breathtaking. The purchases were made a year in advance, which required "knowing the market" in order to recognize a "winner." Certainly my business career was more gratifying than its brief duration might indicate. Such a job offers a sense of purpose, reward, and identity. There are clear goals, a division of responsibility, and well-defined behavior expectations for everyone. Unfortunately, after the initial challenge the way of life itself was not substantially nourishing. The role which at first served as a trellis for my emerging identity became a limitation. Few people wanted to be allies in life, to cooperate, for ultimately the system rewarded competition and power. I was living for my vacations and weekends. Already I had fulfilled my dreams of success, only to discover that it was not accompanied by the satisfaction I had presumed. I wanted more.

Soon after settling in New York City I had renewed my proposal to Nancy Jean Kendig, and we married. Nancy's background was quite different from mine, and she expressed her ideas with conviction and imagination. In contrast to the dogmatism of Catholicism, Nancy's family were religious followers of Emanuel Swedenborg, a sophisticated Christian visionary of the eighteenth century, whose many volumes are studied for their splendid insight. Her interest was biology, the study of life. She gave me a water's-eye view of pond life and later a psychologist's view of human life.

Nancy helped me to realize that both happiness and fulfilling relationships have value for their own sake. She distracted me from my single-minded pursuit of achievement by urging enjoyment, but I found that personal satisfaction is not a goal that can be directly pursued. Happiness is an attitude, a way of being while doing something else, not an end in itself. Unhappiness is a sign that all is not well with the relationships around us. An infant may take his family for granted, but adults must nurture their relationships tenderly. I was surprised to find that, even in business, interpersonal relationships are the most significant, although hidden, items on the agenda. The greatest obstacle to success is the inability to work cooperatively. Again I wondered about the nature of behavior. Nancy and I felt there was more to us than we could give expression to. We both believed that within the world of human experience there awaited greater wisdom. We agreed to search together.

Before we joined the New York Society for Ethical Culture I was clear only about what I did *not* believe. It was an exciting surprise to discover an organization of people who for nearly one hundred years had been doing more than ignoring or opposing popular ideas about life's basic questions. Since I found the Ethical movement, my concept of reality and my understanding of behavior have undergone a metamorphosis.

Most of my current understanding of the world has either evolved or become clearer since my association with the Ethical movement. I have learned things about myself that had not previously been part of my self-image, and I have had practice making my expressions more congruent with my feelings. Although the unconscious mind continually relates to the environment, and thereby has its effect without one's knowledge, I had always assumed that my conscious mind was the totality of me. Now I have a greater awareness of my many dimensions.

Another important contribution to my emerging world-view was the philosophy from which the Ethical movement has grown. Dr. Felix Adler, the original Leader, is little know by present-day members, but his thinking remains the single greatest influence. Dr. Adler observed that all religions shared a concern for righteous living, yet each set its roots in different creeds and traditions. His own mission was to establish a religious organization in which the cultivation of ethics was the highest priority. The cornerstone of his philosophy was his faith in the ability of human beings to act ethically without the supernatural supervision of a godly father. Behavior is not ethical because it fulfills the law of god, but because it best serves the species. If human beings could act in such a way that every individual behavior served perfectly the common good, and therefore every action of society served perfectly its individuals, this would describe the ethical ideal. This is not to suggest a future heaven on earth but merely to offer some non-theistic ground upon which to build an ethical system.

Dr. Adler also understood the need of every individual to experience a sense of purpose. Want of purpose, he observed, was the great ill of societies and individuals. A spiritual perspective gives meaning to our daily trials and breathes energy into our lives.

The basis of all morality, it seems to me, is the assertion that human life is desirable. Each moral system tends to promote behavior which would guarantee the survival of its culture and thereby human life. Each moral system has evolved over time and adopted from others. Unfortunately, this testing of values through their consequences has not become a proper science because cultures have been threatened by the notion that their morality was either relative or evolving. Perhaps it is the strength of our own culture that allows us to both acknowledge its mores and endeavor to change them. Morality, no matter how important, is always relative, for only eternity can evaluate the ultimate outcome: survival. Among mere mortals absolute moral judgments are not possible. This moral realtivity, however, does not relieve us of moral responsibity.

Human life depends upon the ability of people to relate to one another because we are social animals that survive only in groups. Human society is a fabric of interwoven agreements. It can tolerate and benefit from debates over which moral agreements are most necessary, but it will disintegrate if agreements themselves are not respected. Morality, society's consciously and unconsciously agreed upon scheme for survival, is not absolute, but the ability to be moral (to keep agreements) is absolutely necessary. When people fail to respect agreements, their society falters. Therefore, moral responsibility is, first, acknowledging conscious contracts with family, friends, and society; second, realizing that one is also responsible for unconscious agreements which one may become aware of only after they have been broken.

Our behavior will never have the security of absolute moral sanctions, but the study of ethics can lay bare moral premises and make us aware of likely consequences. Since humankind has harnessed such awesome power to destroy, ethics has become increasingly essential. An unconscious morality gone off course may be the cause of our civilization's ultimate catastrophe. Sadly, people who are entrusted with power are not yet chosen for their knowledge of ethics.

Searching for truths by which to live requires belonging to a community that realizes people are continually maturing, a community of people who nourish, stimulate, and discipline one another.

It is a religious experience to be part of something that is larger than all its parts together, to be part of something that depends on you but survives without you. The Ethical movement has been my spiritual and intellectual home. People have channeled me and challenged me. I share the dream of an ethical culture and that dream brings me joy.

REASON, ETHICS, AND RELIGIOUS EXPERIENCE

Michael Eldridge

I HAVE long had an interest in the formulation of an ethical religion that is grounded in ordinary experience and guided not only by its ethical focus but also by critical inquiry. This interest of mine can only be understood by examining my intellectual and religious development.

My parents are members of the Southwest Church of Christ in Oklahoma City. To be a child of theirs was to be a part of this religious community. Three times a week we attended services: Sunday morning, Sunday evening, and Wednesday evening. Our life as a family was all bound up with this sectarian religious community, which was a part of the movement known as the Churches of Christ. The church they read about in the New Testament had no organ or other instrumental music in its worship and no ecclesiastical hierarchy. It baptized only adults, by immersion, and celebrated the Lord's supper every Sunday.

By restoring this New Testament pattern, Alexander Campbell, the nineteenth-century frontier theologian, thought he could unite all of the warring sects into one true church. What happend was that the Campbellites, as they were often called, divided themselves into three groups, the most conservative of which, the Churches of Christ, was particularly prone to controversy and division. Congregations of this movement have split over many issues that would strike most of us as ludicrous: Should one cup or many cups be used in the communion service? If the cups did not have handles, were they glasses and thus not cups? Did the New Testament permit a congregation to organize Bible classes, colleges, or orphan homes? At its worst this doctrinal wrangling was counterproductive legalism, preventing the very unity that Campbell had sought. But as Sydney Ahlstrom, a Yale religious historian, points out, "Campbell was not only a restorationist and a legalist; he was also a fervent exponent of eighteenth-century rationalism, a disciple of John Locke and the Scottish philosophers." For Campbell, said Ahlstrom, faith was "the mind's assent to credible testimony, an emphasis which served powerfully to divorce his movement from the prevailing currents of emotional revivalism. This rationalistic note stands out in his views on baptism," which he viewed as "the decisive, formal compliance of the believer with the command of Jesus, a washing away of sins, not a mysterious supernatural transaction."

There was legalism, devisiveness, controversy, and sectarianism in my religious heritage, but there was also an intense concern to know the will of God and a confidence that I could figure it out by studying the Bible. From early on I was told that New Testament, as opposed to liberal Christianity, was the way to know right from wrong, the answer to life's deepest questions and the only means of salvation from eternal damnation. Consequently, study of the Bible became very important for my life. I majored in Greek and Hebrew in college, expecting to learn God's will for myself. I wanted to get as close as I could to what I perceived to be the record of God's interaction with humanity. One cannot undertake serious study of the Bible without coming into contact with the historical-critical method which insists that one go to the sources, weigh the evidence, and then form conclusions, which in turn are open to testing.

My teachers tried to use the historical method without adopting the relativistic assumptions and conclusions of liberal biblical scholarship. I found, however, that my use of this method led me to share the naturalistic views of the liberal scholars. The Bible, which had been a divinely-inspired book, increasingly came to be viewed by me as a remarkable but human collection of books in which one could trace the development of Israel, Judaism, and the Church. I began my biblical studies with the assumption that the Biblical period was special, unique. I ended with the conclusion that it was no more meaningful than many other historical periods.

One outstanding feature of the biblical collection, nevertheless, is its concern for ethics, personal and social. Justice, mercy, and righteousness are everywhere spoken of. To do God's will is to love Him and one's neighbor. No doubt my life-long concern for ethics springs to a large degree from my biblicistic upbringing and my biblical studies.

This commitment was strengthened by my seminary experience. Not long after entering Yale I was standing in prayer vigils on the New Haven Green with John Smith, a classmate; Roland Bainton, the noted church historian; and others to protest the Vietnam war while passing motorists taunted us with shouts of "Commie cowards!" Christmas 1967 I preached a sermon against American involvement in Vietnam at the Hamden, Connecticut, Church of Christ that shocked and angered the congregation. The following spring I joined hundreds of other Yale students who were working for Eugene McCarthy in the New Haven primary, which we won, beating the local political machine. Later I was active in the New Haven Grape Boycott. Yale was more than courses for me. It was a community where I clarified and reshaped my social ethic of freedom and justice and learned how to express my values in organized protest.

I chose the Yale Divinity School because I wanted the best possible training in biblical and theological studies and because I wanted to get into the mainstream of protestantism. The Churches of Christ were increasingly perceived by me as a sectarian backwater. I wanted to be with people who realized the tension between the biblical period and the twentieth century, not jumping over nineteen centuries as though they were nothing. I had been taught to value the experience of the early Church over all other experience. But the more I studied the more I realized that this history could not be set off to itself. Increasingly I came to rely on my own experience and not on the experience of my nineteenth-century religion's heritage or the biblical experience. Biblical study was fascinating but ultimately less than satisfying in my search for meaning. No matter how much I knew about a particular biblical theme, passage, or word, I still did not know how I was to live. Paul's world was not mine. Israel's history, Jesus' sayings, and Paul's letters had to be qualified, interpreted, and set in context before they had any meaning for today. The need for theology became apparent and I left the biblically-bound churches of Christ for the mainstream of protestantism, looking to liberal Christianity for the answers to my questions of identify, belief, and mission.

Upon graduating from Yale I sought ordination in the Disciples of Christ, the liberal heir to Campbell's restoration movement, thinking that I had personally traversed the same ground which they had corporately traveled. They and I were struggling to live out an historic faith in the contemporary world. I did not find them, however, to be as open to present-day experience as I deemed necessary.

The Disciples did, however, provide me an opportunity to express my social concerns by working in a small ecumenical parish in South Baltimore, a yoked parish made up of a Disciples congregation and a United Church of Christ. For two and a half years I worked in an urban, ethnic, lower middle-class community trying to empower these white but victimized people. I wanted them to know "the full humanity which had been revealed in Jesus of Nazareth" — to use language that was typical of my sermons at the time. While they drew strength from their families and neighborhood, they were threatened by political structures and economic realities which they did not understand and over which they had little control. My community organizing continued when I moved across the harbor to East Baltimore to become pastor of Bethel United Church of Christ. There I was active in a much stronger and more effective group, the Southeast Community Organization.

After awhile I began to wonder: Why was I denying myself in order that my parishioners might experience life in all its fullness? If it was right for them to be saved — by this time I had come to define salvation as a this-worldly experience — then it was right for me also. I had successfully rationalized my Christian heritage with my naturalistic world view. But I could not explain away this anomaly. Why should one deny himself for others? Should not all people work for the well-being of all people? The Christian ethic of self-sacrifice as exemplified in Jesus, the man for others, no longer seemed adequate. There was now no reason for me to remain Christian.

My faith had always been a rational one. As a good Campbellite, I believed something if the evidence and logic compelled me to accept it as true. Since my last semester in seminary, after having been introduced to John Dewey's *A Common Faith*, I had been a naturalist. I had come to value my own experience, no longer viewing the early churches' experience as normative. I had been concerned with ethics for some time, if not all my life. The first decisive factor, however, as I have just related, was that I no longer was willing to deny myself that others might enjoy the good life. The second decisive factor was my finally realizing that as a social activist and naturalistic interpreter of Christianity I was not only out of step with contemporary Christianity but also in conflict with a religion that must always interact with a history of a God who revealed himself in Jesus of Nazareth. No matter how much I might want to de-mytholo-

103

gize this history and re-enact the extracted meaning in our times, I would be rebuked by a majority in the church who would choose to read the story more or less literally and who would refuse to live it out today.

My experience, however, was not one of emptiness, but of liberation. In the process of testing Christianity and finding it deficient, I was, in that very process, defining the kind of faith that would stand the test: an ethical religion that was grounded in ordinary experience and guided not only by its ethical focus but by critical inquiry.

In some ways my discovery of Ethical Culture, the quintessential ethical religion, was accidental. I had resigned from my last pastorate to enter social work. I wanted to work for social justice in the context of a religious community, but I did not know how to do this apart from Christianity. A chance encounter with the Baltimore Ethical Society's president opened up a way for me to act out my religious convictions within a humanistic naturalist framework. Upon investigating this oddly-named Ethical Culture movement I realized that the religion I was constructing in my head had actually been founded by Felix Adler in 1876. All three of the crucial components — reason, ethics, and religious experience — had already come together in the thinking and action of this man.

Although ethical culture, or moral development, was his paramount concern, Adler realized the importance of religious experience and reason. This can be seen in a passage from *Life and Destiny* (in which reason is spoken of as "philosophic thinking"): "All really religious persons declare that religion is, primarily, a matter of experience. We get a certain kind of experience, and then philosophic thinking will be of use to us in explicating what is implicated in that experience. But we must get the experience first." Without the experience there is nothing for reason to work with. Nor is there motivation to act. The experience is primary, but the unreflected-upon experience is not sufficient to guide one's life.

My interest, as I stated at the outset, has been in the formulation of an ethical religion that is grounded in ordinary experience and guided not only by its ethical focus but by critical inquiry. Let me now unpack this statement.

Ethical religion is what Khoren Arisian, an Ethical Leader in New York City, has defined as "a sense of lively connectedness with the world." But it is, in my judgment, more than this. It is also the experience which occasions this sense and the actions that are shaped by it. The actions, in turn, are new experience which occasion a new sense of lively connectedness. Some would say that the only experiences that are truly religious in character are those which are ecstatic in some other-worldly sense. I think, however, that any experience which enables one to know that he is a part of this world related not only to other human beings, but to the total environment, is religious in character.

In *A Common Faith* John Dewey speaks of the empirical method in this fashion: "There is but one sure road of access to truth — the road of patient, cooperative inquiry operating my means of observation, experiment, record and controlled reflection." He refers to the method of the natural sciences, but this method cannot be readily transferred to the study of dynamic institutions, movements, causes, and individuals. We can, however, observe and analyze people and events, experiences and beliefs, asking, Is this insight life-supporting? Does it promote a sense of belonging in the universe? Does it square with our understanding of the world? If it does not, which needs modification — our new insight or our world-view? There must be a constant interplay between observation, analysis, and new understanding. Conceived in this way there is a role for the empirical method in religious experience.

Let me now illustrate this by relating a personal experience and reflecting on it.

In the fall of 1975 Cesar Chavez, president of the United Farm Workers (UFW), visited a work camp of one of the major California lettuce producers. Outside the dining hall, according to *The New York Times*, Chavez spoke to about 100 workers, passionately urging them to vote for the UFW in an election made possible by California's new farm legislation. Chavez addressed the *campesinos* (field workers) in Spanish:

"The campesino has to decide this election by himself. No one else can do it for him. The teamsters use fear. Do not be afraid. If the farm industry is not dominated by one union, it will always have the unions fighting each other instead of the grower. We are all campesinos and we should get together and work together. The U.F.W. is more than just a union — it's liberty and people. This is the most important decision of your life."

I read this statement in *The Times* while riding the bus to my office. Struck by the phrases, ". . . more than a union . . . liberty and people . . . most important decision of your life," I began to sob silently, following which came the awareness that this was a religious experience.

I identify with people who are engaged in the struggle for liberty, who band together to bring about well-being for themselves and others. To experience solidarity with those who are working for social justice is, for me, a religious experience. Life becomes more worthwhile when I sense that there are others who are working for social justice, willing to pursue, in Dewey's description of religious commitment, "an ideal end against obstacles and in spite of threats of personal loss because of conviction of its general and enduring value."

But is Chavez's statement an accurate one? It is not enough to be moved by his words and to realize that my reaction is consistent with my convictions about social justice? I must also inquire into the facts of the matter. Religious experience is not divorced from the world of empirically-verifiable facts.

In this case we may well ask: Is the UFW worthy of support? Does it live up to its rhetoric? Will the well-being of farmworkers and others be enhanced by its efforts? Just because we are moved by the words *liberty and people* does not mean we can forbid our intelligence from critically examinging the experience. Intelligence, however, is not a process which Ethical Culturists reluctantly allow to examine religious experience. On the contrary, we welcome the use of intelligence in our efforts to bring about well-being. Only by critically examining our experiences and modifying our beliefs can we possess attitudes that, in Dewey's words, truly "Lend deep and enduring support to the processes of living." Only by critical inquiry can we develop our experiences into attitudes and actions that reflect a sense of lively connectedness with the world and are thus both religious and ethical. Critical inquiry enables us to develop an ethical religion that is grounded in ordinary experience.

The tragedy of life is not that we are unable to fulfill our visions but that we are able to do so. The Holocaust was not an accident. It was the logical outcome of Hitler's racist vision. As the prize-winning documentary about the Vietnam War, *Hearts and Minds*, painfully but vividly makes clear, Vietnam was not a quagmire into which we stumbled, but the inevitable result of America's cold-war mentality. We must not turn away from reason or stop seeing visions. We must instead *use* our intelligence to shape our visions into worthy attitudes that will promote the life processes.

As a movement that finds its purpose in the education of morally autonomous persons, Ethical Culture enables me as one of its Leaders to influence hearts and minds. I have been a religious professional. I have been a social activist. I have been a teacher.

SPIRITUALITY: THE FORGOTTEN FACTOR

Jean Somerville Kotkin

POETS HAVE been called "the antennae of the human race," a phrase that would apply equally well to novelists and playwrights. Literary works bring into sharper focus the religious significance of the deeper themes of life, such as the human's search for a soul, for comradeship, for inner peace, for a place in the cosmos, for hope for creative satisfaction. It is an odd paradox that just as religious dogmas were being relaxed through the liberalizing movements of the late nineteenth and twentieth centuries, the literary world should have been renewing these and making them a point of appeal.

There is a curious hiatus that has arisen between people of letters and people of faith which has made for a deplorable lack of understanding and communication between these groups. Many theologians and clergy feel today that they have no clarity regarding the spiritual insights to be found in our best literature; indeed, they are frequently confused and bewildered by it, often writing it off as a prime example of the confusion and bewilderment discernible everywhere in the realm of spirit today. And similarly, there are many otherwise credible literary people whose knowledge of what is taking place in theology today is almost sublimely unenlightened. Their creative works are therefore legitimate but uninformed fumbling after solutions to problems of the spirit. Where esthetic skill and theological awareness meet, as in poets such as T. S. Eliot and W. H. Auden, a poetry of unusual penetration and genius results. And where the theologians possess also some understanding of the interpretive significance of the arts, as in the works of Paul J. Tillich or Gabriel Marcel, a superior penetration into the religious mysteries appears.

Many writers have tried to explain the search for the soul through categories of space, time, and logic. However, I feel that the essence of the human does not exist within these categories. There is the unexplained something that Rudolph Otto calls "the wholly other"; that Sinclair Lewis refers to as that "faint and uncertain inkling of something which one is born desiring"; that Seigfried Sassoon terms "the stillness where the spirits walk and all but inmost faith is overthrown." Somerset Maugham as an old man wrote in his journal, "I think that there is in the heroic courage with which man confronts the irrationality of the world a beauty greater than the beauty of art . . . . There is a nobility that which does not proceed from thoughts. It is more elemental. It depends neither on culture nor breeding. It has roots among the most primitive instincts in the human being. Faced with it, God, if he created man, might hang his head in shame."

Whatever the majesty of the words, the beauty of the poetry, whatever our modernity, there remains that before which our tongues fall silent, before which we stand in awe. It is the moment when the concert is ended and both the audience and the players in the orchestra listen to the vibrating silence before the applause begins.

How does all this apply to Ethical Culture? What we in the movement teach is that within each man and woman lives the sacred — that even if we were stripped of all possessions, all power, all pretense, there would still be that trusted center of sanctity. Not because anyone or anything bestowed it upon us, but because that sacred element lies at the core of what it means to be human.

The preclassical and classical Greeks symbolized the hidden aspects of human nature, in particular the forces that motivated people to perform memorable deeds, by the word *entheos* — a god within. From *entheos* is derived *enthusiasm*. People today may no longer believe in the divine origin of inspiration, but there are few who do not retain the ancient mystical faith that enthusiasm is a source of creativity. Whatever religious or philosophical allegiance one has, there would be few to deny that there would be little chance of improving the world if it were not for the faith derived from the god within.

In the original Greek sense, the word *enthusiasm* meant far more than deep interest, ardént zeal, or twinkling eyes. It implied "divine madness," the mania that Socrates regarded as the mainspring of all worthwhile creations. It suggests that logic and clear thinking do not entirely account for the creative manifestations of human life. Scientists, artists, administrators, reformers have acknowledged that their most valuable ideas and achievements have emerged spontaneously from the subconscious region of their minds. Plato stated this in *Phaedrus:* "In reality, the greatest of blessings comes to us through madness, when it's sent as a gift of the gods . . . madness which comes from the gods, is superior to sanity, which is of human origin."

Even René Descartes, champion of the purest form of rationalism, reported that his famous method originated during a dreamlike state over which he had no control. He wrote in his journal: "10 November 1619, when I was full of enthusiasm, and I discovered the fundamental principles of a wonderful knowledge." Subconscious inspiration, rather than orderly methodic thought, was primarily responsible for the "Discours sur la Methode."

Ideals and commitments are the expression of entheos, the god within each of us, which accounts for the emergence and governance of our thoughts and actions.

After a conversation in Amsterdam in 1950 with Martin Buber, Dr. Matthew Ies Spetter, the Leader of the Riverdale-Yonkers Ethical Society, made the following note of what Buber had said: "The essential struggle of our time is the struggle of the human spirit against all that which is subhuman. Many aspects of the subhuman have already made it more difficult to listen to the inner human voice. And when we cannot hear we cannot answer." Our struggle today in Ethical Culture is to hear, and listen to that inner voice.

When the movement was founded over 100 years ago, there were three main thrusts: education, social action, and religion. Our Schools in New York are in fine shape. The social actions started by the Ethical Societies of New York, Chicago, Philadelphia, and St. Louis have left an indelible mark on the life and habits of those cities in terms of settlement houses, visiting nurses, adult education, youth work, racial unity, and prison reform. It is in the religious area that I am most troubled. We have all the trappings, the meeting houses, and Leaders, the programs, the Sunday schools, which are all over the country.

However, in my travels around the United States to other Societies, and even in the New York Society, there seems to be a lack of a central sense of purpose. What we need is a spiritual revival; that is, we need to set operating in people a new or renewed spiritual principle. If you want to run an electric railroad you have to build a power house and supply energy. It is this lack of energy, lack of spirituality that is complained about by the smaller Societies in the movement. We are always assuming the ethical motives and supposing that all we need to do is to arouse them, bring them into action. It just doesn't work that way. The motives have to be built up day after day; and to this end a new spiritual principle must be evoked in people. As Felix Adler wrote many years ago:

> I can merely say that without an intense moral faith there can be no moral fervor, and that if there is to be a new upward turn in ethics and religion, if Ethical Societies are to multiply, they cannot be made to do so by instituting forum lectures, by devising a ritual, or even by establishing social settlements and other good works, however indispensable these may be; but that the Movement must give birth to personalities who have attained for themselves an abiding ethical faith, and are aflame with it, that the extension of the Movement depends on the rise of a succession of such personalities to hand on the torch from one to the other. Mohammed, it is said, secured his first success by converting his wife. The great task of the ethical teacher is to convert himself. If he has done that thoroughly, down to the core of his being, he will convert others.

It is only the appeal to the highest in people that has ever produced results. It was not the people who pleaded for more humane treatment of the blacks in the south who accomplished their delivery, but those who worked for the abolition of slavery. At that time it seemed an impossible dream. Yet we have seen results. The same thing was true when dedicated older people and young students rallied to the South to establish voting rights and civil rights for Blacks in the Fifties and Sixties. It was people who found a spiritual principle of total renovation who moved and changed the face of this land.

René Dubos, the eminent microbiologist, feels that humans, when they lost touch with nature, lost touch with their sense of inner being. And in losing touch with their inner self they became more and more alienated and lonely.

The idea of god or gods has served humans through the ages as a picture or an image enabling them to think the thought of this vast endless universe. The idea of the unity of a universe of countless worlds has been too mind-boggling for humans to grasp and they invented gods to explain, gods to blame, gods to fear, gods to supplicate, gods to worship since time immemorial. With the advent of scientific advances, people had a new god to worship — science. Once the hope of mankind, modern science has now become the object of such mistrust and disappointment that it will probably never speak again with its old authority. The crisis of ecology, the threat of atomic war, and the disruption of the patterns of human life by advanced technology have all eroded what was once a general trust in the goodness of science. With the spiritual revolution that has taken place among the young, with the introduction to them of new religions sourced in the East, people today are searching for a new world-view. A sure sign that this movement is more than a youthful fad is the fact that lately many scientists, our chief representatives of modern culture, have begun to look to the teachings of Eastern and Western mystics for new visions of the cosmos.

Jacob Needlemen, in his essay, "Modern Man Between Two Worlds," which is part of his recent book, *A Sense of the Cosmos*, states:

> For several centuries Western civilization has operated under the assumption that man can understand the universe without understanding himself. But having turned the available energy of our minds toward the external world, we now find ourselves more perplexed and anxious than ever in front of a reality that simply will not yield to our hopes and desires . . . . Now — fitfully and with great uncertainty — it seems that we are all called back from the impulse to believe we can stride into nature with our mind pointed outward like an unsheathed sword. Both within and outside the sciences a new sense of the unknown has appeared. The unknown is ourselves.

He goes on to say that the premise of his book is that Western civilization, as a whole, now finds itself between dreams. In that fleeting state between dreams which is called despair in some Western teachings and self-questioning in Eastern traditions, people are said to be able to receive the truth, both about nature and their own possible role in the universal order. Throughout the ages, the hidden psychological methods of ancient traditions have operated to guide people in that state between dreams, where a person can begin the long and difficult work of self-investigation leading to transformation.

Why are we so afraid of the word *spirituality* in the Ethical movement today? It was used with ease and dedication by Felix Adler as part of countless talks: "The Spiritual Attitude Toward our Neighbors," "Spiritual Self-Education," "The Meaning of Temperance as an Aid to Spiritual Life," to name just a few. Perhaps what we should look at is what it means in an Ethical Culture context. As usual, it is easier to say what it does *not* mean. It does not mean living through with others their upward or downward course — that is a sympathetic, not a spiritual, relationship. Ordinary human love is that which desires the success of another, another's health, prosperity, intellectual and cognate achievements — while spiritual love cannot but contemplate the inevitable defeat of the beloved person; the defeat in health, inevitable at the end; the defeat in mental achievement, because every mental achievement is faulty; the defeat in character development, because every character remains broken.

"To live in the life of others" is an ambiguous phrase. To me it means I live in the effort, the striving to produce in the other a certain consciousness, namely that the real self is not the one that has failed. The consciousness that is the real self is invincible, unbroken. I live in the act of calling it out of its depth. I live in my faith in it. I become active spiritually as I achieve a sense of the spiritual linkage with the other, aware of our natures being so interlaced and interwoven that I can become a true entity as I lift this other being out of the stream of change and produce in the other being the same sense of linkage as I experience myself.

Spirit is one of the potencies of being. The definition of the spiritual nature of the human from an ethical point of view is the unique excellence of every fellow human being. Look for it, regard him or her as an individual; treat him or her as such; help him or her become more and more his or her own spiritual self; elicit the best in him or her. That is what is meant to stand in spiritual relationship to another human; so to influence people as to bring out, as to create, this personality in them. You will have to call out from the depths of your being the best in you, and the best in you will greet the best in the other; the spiritual nature in you and in the other will rise to the surface in the same act, as the product of the same effort.

The real greatness of man shows itself only when the heroic spirit is most challenged. And we are all of us capable of more than we ordinarily suppose. There are depths upon depths in us that we are never aware of until we face unafraid the difficulties we imagine we can never bear. It is marvelous what can be done by courage, which is only strength made conscious of its unused resources. The Ethical faith believes that the spirit of man, awake and aware of itself, is more than a match for whatever it is called upon to meet.

A SPIRITUAL AUTOBIOGRAPHY

Paul R. Migliore

MOST OF us in the Ethical movement, whether as professional Leaders or as members, have come to Ethical humanism as our basic religious commitment from one of the traditional religions. Of course, after a century some have grown up within the movement and as adults may have joined one of its Societies. Yet since we conceive of membership in an Ethical Society as a mature life decision, as a very specific and conscious act of commitment, it does not mean that one is automatically a member of the Ethical movement.

For all of us, members and non-members alike, identification with the Ethical philosophy represents a milestone in our own spiritual and religious development. Some who have joined Ethical Societies scorn the word *religion* and shun altogether terms like *religious* or *spiritual commitment* to describe their feelings. Many others still strongly identify with the cultural heritage of the religion into which they were born. Clearly, most people in the Ethical movement have migrated from the temples and churches to establish themselves in a new home with a new philosophy. And though our backgrounds are quite diverse and our own individual preferences of taste or emphasis differ, we have gathered together under one spiritual and philosophical roof called Ethical humanism.

Our spiritual autobiographies reveal the process of evolution and maturation that each of us has undergone. Our individual and collective understanding of this process is critical in a humanist philosophy which holds that we develop our humanity through our involvement with others in community. The process of resolving our inner struggles of conscience and our conflicts with popular values, traditions, and their institutional representatives, is part of the measure of our development as morally autonomous individuals — presumably the life goal (if there is one) of an Ethical humanist philosophy. Though the process is lifelong, there are milestones which we can see when we look back along the path which we have traversed.

I was raised without formal religious training in a family which was the product of a mixed marriage between a Catholic and a Jew. My father, who was raised as a Catholic in Italy, has long since turned his back on Catholicism. It would be fair to say he does not have a single kind word to say about the Roman Church. The residue of bitterness he feels is a phenomenon not uncommon among ex-Catholics and presumably explains, at least to some extent, why Italy has the largest Communist Party in Western Europe. As children growing up in Phoenix, Arizona, the only religious tradition we ever caught a glimpse of was that of Judaism. My mother, like many Jews, holds a strong sense of identification with the culture into which she was born, though she does not relate to Judaism in a religious sense. Our limited exposure to Judaism was essentially a by-product of our association with the then small Jewish community which tended to band together as the only oasis of intellectual concern in Phoenix in the late 1940s and early 1950s.

As children we were neither encouraged nor discouraged from inquiring about religion. We were not trotted around to various religious organizations and told that at some point in our lives we should make a choice for ourselves. Rather, religion in any formal sense was just not present in our environment. Instead we were brought up in a household with strong humanist values. We lived in a family where social consciousness was acute. We discussed values and issues and were encouraged to develop and test our own ideas and perceptions. Our opinions were solicited, our views shared with adults in discussions, to be accepted or rejected on their merits as they would be from any participant. We were neither patronized nor catered to. The decision whether or not to participate was ours.

One's own development of a personal spiritual philosophy comes out of life experience and falls into patterns at a very early age, though not always consciously. I suppose to the extent that I came from a socially conscious family in which questions of right and wrong, justice, truth, and values were verbalized openly, I had more awareness of their relative influence in my environment than perhaps other children. Not that I saw more than anyone else, but I always thought about what I saw in terms of right and wrong, justice and injustice, humanity and inhumanity.

In Phoenix, when I was very young, my family lived on the grounds of a tuberculosis sanitarium which was part of an Indian Reservation for Navajo and Apache Indians. From my earliest memories I knew the sights of poverty, oppression, and intolerance long before I understood them. Then, as a pre-teenager, I moved to Austin, Texas, where I enrolled in the neighborhood junior high school, an all-white segregated school (despite the 1954 Supreme Court decision).

Austin in the mid-1950s was still a legally segregated community. I remember the "Whites Only" signs on drinking fountains and rest rooms. Blacks lived on the "other" side of town, went to their own schools, and stayed in their own community. My only contact with blacks while living in the South was the occasional domestics in the homes of more affluent schoolmates. I clearly remember the atmosphere of white racism that permeated my school. I'll never forget a discussion at lunch one day when the ex-Governor's son said to me, "Would you play football with a 'nigger' on the other side of the line?" Or my eighth-grade American history class where I got into a long debate with the teacher who taught us that slavery was a benevolent institution. It could not have oppressed blacks, she argued, because there was nothing to be gained by harming someone for whom you had just paid $1200!

When I was fourteen years old my family spent a month driving through the remote villages and major cities of Mexico. The poverty I witnessed then — people living in three-sided stick lean-tos with mud floors and no furnishings, children in skimpy, tattered clothes with no shoes, a man literally lying dead in the street in Cuernavaca — made a very deep impression on me. And so, too, did the murals and frescos of Jose Clemente Orózco, painted in small chapels and several public buildings in central Mexico, portraying the revolutionary struggles of the Mexican people.

Two other things from that trip had an influence on me. The first was seeing the remains of several statues of prominent Americans surrounded by high metal enclosures after having been blown up by Mexican students on the campus of the University of Mexico. The second was attending a bull fight (which was jarring enough), sitting in the very first row and seeing the matador severely gorred not thirty feet away. Between each fight they would roll out a ten-foot high Coca-Cola bottle from one side of the arena as an advertisement while they dragged the bloody carcass of the bull out the other side behind a team of horses. The impression that has lasted with me from that trip was of the worst products of human nature: poverty, oppression, and sadism. But I was also impressed by the people of conscience leading the revolutionary struggles, people with enormous spiritual energy who refused to accept such things as reality.

From my earliest involvement in political action as a young teenager, I have never acted out any singular ideological commitment. Rather, my perceptions, my critique, and my action flow fundamentally out of very strongly held, quite personal, idealistic and humanistic commitments whose roots can be traced back to my early life. At times the end products of social and political action motivated by religious commitment are hard to distinguish from those motivated by ideological commitment. Two people can speak out against oppression for very different reasons, yet still oppose the same thing. Indeed we often refer glibly to the religiosity of political activists because their manner often resembles that of religious zealots. Both religion and political ideology are often animated by deep emotional energy.

Because my political philosophy is an outgrowth of my own personal spiritual commitment and flow organically out of my own life experience as I have interpreted it and not out of ideological constructs created by political philosophers, I do not see politics in terms of the working out of a universal dialectic. Thus, my political judgments need be only consistent with my conscience, and not with any political, economic, or social theory. To the extent that I am a morally autonomous individual, I feel obliged only to satisfy my own conscience and not the discipline of this or that political line. To the extent that I am motivated by a humanist consciousness which flows from my inner religious spirit, I am more flexible and more open than if I were motivated solely by ideology.

In early 1961 I transferred from my segregated junior high school in Austin to an integrated New York public high school where whites comprised a thirty percent minority among mostly blacks and Hispanic students. Most of my classmates came from working class families, though among the whites were a handful with middle class backgrounds. Many among the whites were Irish or Italian Catholics who had left the parochial schools. Others were recent European immigrants who spoke very little English.

Given the diverse backgrounds of my classmates and the many "progressive" teachers with whom we came into contact, the early 1960s in New York City was for me a time of intense political and social involvement. We had chapters of CORE, SNCC, and student SANE in school. We marched together with the community to resist the havoc and dislocation the building of Lincoln Center was creating in the neighborhood. We marched to support the teachers when they reorganized their union in the early 1960s. And there were the annual Easter peace walks to "Ban the Bomb," and rallies near the U.N., along with the early peace marches on Washington before Vietnam had become a popular issue. And somewhere along the line I saw Eleanor Roosevelt speak from the back of a flatbed truck at a street corner political rally.

My political involvement during those years along with my social awareness as a youngster were fundamental to my own evolutionary journey to Ethical humanism. A humanist's spiritual autobiography is the biography of commitment. However, not until I came to work on the staff of the New York Society for Ethical Culture, prior to entering as a Leader-in-training, did I become acquainted in any systematic intellectual sense with the philosophy of the movement. I had already formulated my own personal humanist position. Since that time I have come to make the equations between my own philosophy and that of the Ethical movement, translating my own commitments into the language of religious commitment, a language with which I had no real previous experience.

I have come to hold Ethical humanism as my religious commitment without having brought along any negative emotional baggage in reaction against earlier religious training. Yet in my own journey I do share certain things in common with those who are neither comfortable with calling the Ethical movement a religion nor describing their own humanist commitment as a religious one.

Let me explain why. While in high school I was introduced to the National Ethical Youth Organization, the youth group of the Ethical movement. It was not run as a recruitment ground for the Ethical Societies, but as a service for young people in the community. In the course of my high school years I first became the local and then the national president of the NEYO group at a time when it had over a thousand members located in virtually every Society in the movement.

Because I was the president of NEYO, I spent a great deal of time at the New York Society with the staff and Leaders and at neighboring Societies as well. Long before I had any formal sense of the movement's philosophy, I came intuitively to know what it was about by being at the Society, working with and among the people there, and seeing in practice what "Ethical" meant. In a less formal way the NEYO groups really functioned like mini-Ethical Societies, even down to having a Sunday Platform at the weekend conferences. In the discussion groups the young people wrestled with all the difficult moral questions of interpersonal relations, philosophy, society, politics, and the world order.

In the summers of 1964 and 1965 I participated in the Encampment of Citizenship, first in Puerto Rico and then at the Fieldston School in New York with Allard Lowenstein. We met socialist Norman Thomas; we heard folk singer Peter Seeger; we had discussions with Juan Bosch of the Dominican Republic; and we lived together as students from around the world — people of all races and creeds. Again, I was learning what this Ethical movement was about by being a part of what it did. I became saturated with its philosophy in action; it permeated by being because it reinforced what I had already come to believe.

Invariabley all people test religion against their individual experience. But because Ethical humanism is a religious philosophy which grows directly out of individual and collective experience, its manifestations are as significant to it as creeds are to traditional religion. When we as Ethical humanists respond most genuinely out of the commitments which lie deep within us, we respond with the same quality of commitment which traditionalists easily identify for themselves as religious. Because for me "religion" does not involve a negative connotation from an earlier time in life, I do not feel uncomfortable adopting such language to describe what is indeed within me. My commitments are just as meaningful and just as sacred as anyone else's within the moral universe.

A religious movement does not exist in its creeds or philosophy, for they only serve to clarify and explicate it. A religious movement exists in its adherents, in the people who give it life and flesh, who in the course of their lives attempt to live out its moral philosophy and strive to reach the ideals it prescribes. For any religious movement it is imperative that it be clear about its source of moral energy and commitment. Without elaborate theological constructs, Ethical humanists find their source of moral energy and seek the fruition of its spirit in life's experience, in their relationships with their fellow beings, with nature, the cosmos, and their own individual consciences.

This ethical philosophy of life is dynamic. It exists only in its animated state, and thus we often call it a living faith. The Ethical movement grows historically and philosophically out of both

Judaism and Christianity. But it developed as part of American liberal religion as a new religious movement indebted to, yet quite distinctive from, its philosophical and historical forebears. Still, the fact of its historical and philosophic continuity with American religious liberalism is not the source of the legitimacy of its claim to define itself rightfully as a religion just as valid and genuine and profound as traditional religion. We need not feel the necessity of trying to justify that claim to anyone.

A PHILOSOPHY OR A FREE COMMUNITY?

Howard Box

It will be the glory of our generation if we shall succeed in founding a human religion, a pure faith, a pure religious spirit, born of thought, but of a thought embodying life and fertile of new life.

— Benedetto Croce,
Italian philosopher (1866-1952)

ETHICAL CULTURE should take its future seriously, and it should seriously endeavor to lay claim to a larger role in American life than it has had before. Now, for the first time, there are voices from many places calling out for a religious life rooted in the humanistic perspective. A recent television series has made almost a household word of the name Jacob Bronowski, one of the greatest philosophers of humanism and of ethics in ours, or any, age. Sarvepalli Radhakrishnan, a former president of India, described his own religious proposals as "scientific, empirical and humanistic." There is a lively dialogue proceeding in publication and, when possible, in person between Marxist humanists and "Western" humanists. There is a formal dialogue in existence now between Roman Catholics and the world humanist movement, of which we are a part. Even the brief "Death of God" movement of the last decade, whatever its con-

121

fusions, was evidence of the increasing seriousness with which the religious community takes the challenge of humanist thought. All this suggests that a new humanistic age in religion is about to dawn, and that we have been harbingers of the new way and can now hope to influence its development.

Yet if we are to have a significant future, and an effective program to reach that future, we must try to resolve at least one important issue that has clouded much of our history. Our future depends on what choice we make between two ideas that have been widely held throughout the movement during all of its history. Up to now, neither idea has succeeded in becoming predominant, and the movement has been at least confused, and perhaps seriously injured, by the conflicting counsel that is presented in the two different approaches.

The first idea is that we represent an organized philosophy. It is easy to think of the Ethical movement as a philosophy because it has been for most of its history influenced by the philosophy of Dr. Felix Adler, whose activities created the movement in 1876. His own philosophy, essentialy an unchanging one, was elaborated from *Creed and Deed*, which offered selected addresses from the first year of the movement, through *An Ethical Philosophy of Life* in 1918, on to *The Reconstruction of the Spiritual Ideal* in 1923. For an intellectual world in which traditional religion could no longer be affirmed, he proposed a "spiritual ideal," a faith in the ever-enriching development of the human individual and of society. If this conception was not rooted in a God, and Dr. Adler most emphatically avoided the term, it was nevertheless rooted in the universe and reflected the firm meta-physics of Immanuel Kant. So we are forced to say that his position was markedly different from any of the philosophies that might be called contemporary humanism.

It is helpful to me in thinking of Dr. Adler's position to recall that it was his faith that there was within all men the value sense, a conscience or a consciousness that illumined ethics. And by this the individual was led to the judgment that man is an end *per se*, to use the language of Kant. Dr. Adler saw this as "the force which penetrates into conscousness, that works, that moves, that influences," from which the normative rule of life could be derived. Perhaps the position can be made clearer by quoting from *The Reconstruction of the Spiritual Ideal*, in which Dr. Adler says, "there are metaphysical powers that work in what Freudians call the subconscious even in the case of those who are least aware of them." In these terms it was then possible to see all men potentially marching together down the evolving halls of time, as self-conscious citizens of a "spiritual universe."

This was no fly-by-night radicalism and offered in no sense an easier moral burden than the traditional faiths. It was emphatically a responsible liberalism that sustained a genuinely ethical enthusiasm, as the efforts of the movement showed in its schools and its settlement houses and in the myriad other things that it endeavored to do for the suffering city in which it was born. We can continue to see this as a noble vision, in part because it does allow for the great diversity which we now represent. The human ideal for Dr. Adler was itself a developed variety of responses. In this sense and in many others all of us will continue to be deeply influenced by the vision of Felix Adler.

With so rich a background in philosophy, and with so attractive a figure at the center of the movement, it is easy to see why many people look upon us as a philosophy. However, there are problems in such a conception. I fear the truth today is that few people understand the philosophy of Dr. Adler. The mind of this generation does not readily turn to "philosophical idealism." Both scientific philosophy and existentialism, the two major schools of the present, arose in opposition to the idealism of Kant. Such thoughts are no longer "in the air." And however great an admiration there is for Dr. Adler within the movement, I know of no leader who would claim to be his follower in philosophy. I think we will continue to find certain of Dr. Adler's ideas helpful, but as a system it is not a contemporary alternative. And this has long been true. Nevertheless, this has not stopped us from talking and sometimes acting as if we were in the business of developing and promoting a "philosophy."

Fortunately, there has been a second idea which has been no less firmly established with us. This idea suggests that we are a free meeting house — a center for the individual quest for human values, for the meanings of life, and for the good of all. This assumes that we must each proceed in our own way and at our own rate of travel and it assumes also that we will differ on many issues, including the issues at stake in philosophy. This idea invites us to become a dramatic mixture of forum and temple and to create a way of life that is potentially open to all men. Its key will be not so much the affirmation of principles as the guarantee of an atmosphere of freedom in which the individual may live and think and act. Here is one way it has been expressed:

> The freedom of thought is a sacred right of every individual
> man . . . . Believe or disbelieve as ye list — we shall in all times

respect any honest conviction — but be one with us where there is nothing to divide — in action.

The words are from Dr. Adler's first year of addresses, from the book *Creed and Deed*. Surely they reflect a very different idea from any assumption that he was organizing a philosophy or what some might call a philosophical group. Here is the conception of a community of concern and study and action. Action for this movement in its early decade meant philanthropy, kindergartens, mothers' study groups, visiting nurses, as well as the more famous Schools and settlement houses. However, action also meant what we now call "public affairs," including the public statements that are the forerunners of our resolutions and many other forms of leadership and pressure in public life that would today be called "social action" in other religious circles.

Though he worked and wrote from his own very clear philosophy, Dr. Adler collected around him men who were themselves very different from him and from one another — men such as William Macintyre Salter, who was able to write what was almost an Ethical liturgy, and Alfred W. Martin, who proposed the "symphony of the religions" and interpreted the Ethical movement as an approach toward this kind of religious syncretism. I believe that in putting forward the phrase "not by the Creed, but by the Deed" in his first address, Dr. Adler was very consciously creating what I have called the "free meeting house." And the movement went on to hear the great Americans of that time, like William James, and to be influenced, sometimes despite Dr. Adler, by Freud and Dewey, Russell, Sartre, Camus, and others. In fact we have been a very good example of the free meeting house, and I approve of this direction. However, I do note that we have not always realized that this is our nature.

These two ideas which we have held of the movement continue to exist now and continue to be in tension with one another. They pull us in opposite directions.

If we are a philosophy, then it is easy to see that we have an inside truth to protect and that we should do so. It would clearly follow that we should carefully screen and indoctrinate our members, that we should keep the elder members on our boards, that we should brush aside those who momentarily agree with us on external issues but do not share our philosophy, that we should discourage as members those who might be attracted by our social stand or our organizational advantages. If we are a philosophy we will get clear directions for the movement from the philosophy and not from outside sources or forces.

On the other hand, *if we are a free community*, then the truth is outside and everywhere and we have nothing to protect. If we are a free community, we are all searching (or, to put it more cynically, guessing about life and the universe). And it would seem obvious that we should welcome the widest range of persons and expect to learn from all of them, that we should seek new inspiration and fresh voices and even fresh issues and problems, that we whould expect to be continually redirected by events and by philosophical thrusts from the outside and from the worlds of religion, art, and culture. It would seem to follow that even the ethics of one decade then will not necessarily be those of the next, though our free search for the truth will include the search for the truth that informs choice.

I am sure for some people it will seem at first glance that there is no necessary problem between the desire for a philosophy and the desire for a free meeting house and a "free community," itself the very phrase that is used by one of the European members of the International Humanist and Ethical Union. But on a closer look there is much involved in the distinction. It is the choice between the closed and the open in an organization, between the settled confidence and the energetic search, between the small fellowship and the group, whatever its size, which senses itself as a reflection of a world community. I think the dinstinction that I am making is similar to that between the book on one hand and the whole library on the other. The appeal for many of us in the Ethical movement is that it promises to come down more concretely and more firmly and more dramatically than anyone has before with the idea of the religious society as a genuinely free fellowship. Certainly this has been true through most of our history, despite the confusion that the philosophical approach has engendered.

Does this mean that I am suggesting that philosophy be banned? Is there to be no place in the future for philosophical discussion? No. We will continue to have much discussion of philosophy; we will in fact have more discussion as more people of different opinions are drawn into the Ethical movement. And certainly we should be hospitable toward all those men and women with responsible positions that prevent them from feeling at home in the traditional framework of church or synagogue. And I trust we will continue to use the diversity of the Sunday morning Platform as a way of regularly hearing outsiders, as well as a way of talking to ourselves.

The truth is that our past offers something more important for our future than a philosophy. What was really launched in 1876 was a new concept of the church and synagogue, not as a community of agreement, but as a fellowship of differentiation and exploration and construction — the construction of ideas and of institutions, and of people. We emerge as the idealistic community of free men united in a free search for the truth (including that truth which informs choice, which is at least the beginning of an "ethic") and in a free commitment to what Dr. Adler called "ethical experience."

Our clarification of ourselves as a "free community" — as a fellowship welcoming all truth, and welcoming as well all those purposes and causes and hopes which have been called *ideals* — will help to answer some of the other issues before us. What kind of public image do we seek? What kind of projects or new groups should we launch? What kind of leadership should we encourage? To whom is our message addressed, with what intended effect? What do we want to issue from this movement?

The definition of our movement in terms of "community" seems to open a wide, useful role full of potentialities for future development. Much of the thinking about this is still ahead of us, but here is a statement that seems appropriate to this observer at this time:

> We are a free community seeking the truth in our freedom and finding it primarily in humanist thought and in our own *ethical experience*. On these bases we are reconstructing a group religious life in which we offer one another inspiration, support, education, and the opportunity to express our emerging ideals in the larger society of mankind by example, service, and social action. This idea for a new religious community is ultimately addressed to all humanity, but realistically it is addressed to the domestic scene in the expectation of a more significant "human religion" still to emerge from the existing Ethical, American Humanist, and Unitarian Universalist organizations.

Another way to express this, perhaps, is to say that we are a movement within American liberal religion — as we undoubtedly were at the time of our founding with Dr. Adler's parallel involvement with the Free Religious Association. I would say that we are the most attractive "model" for religious life to come out of that period. And this judgment has much to do with my seeking to serve in the Ethical movement after a decade's experience as an active Unitarian minister. Yet it certainly seems that the idea of the Ethical society has been most influential in exactly the liberal churches of what is now the Unitarian Universalist Association. Perhaps only someone who has kept close ties with both movements, as I have, can be aware of this, but it seems to me that the great success of the humanistic perspective in the Unitarian world is itself a triumph of the *idea* of an Ethical society.

For the future I hope that the Ethical movement will be prepared to learn from other movements, and at the same time feel confident that they will learn much from us. The process will enhance their future *and* ours. The exchange, if we will pursue it, may help all of us respond to and gain from the dawning of a new humanistic age.

EXISTENTIAL HUMANISM: A MINORITY VIEWPOINT

Kenneth J. Smith

FOR PRACTICALLY every Ethical Leader from the beginning, myself included, there must be a religious dimension to our Ethical humanism, else we fail. It is of significance that humanistic psychologists agree, and that such celebrated figures as Carl Jung and Erich Fromm believe that the lack of a religious dimension is a prime cause of neurosis. Erich Fromm, in his book, *The Revolution of Hope*, goes so far as to say that people can go insane without an adequate orientation of meaning: "Man would indeed go mad if he did not find a frame of reference enabling him to feel at home and escape the experience of utter helplessness, disorientation, and uprootedness."

Every person's life, then, can be interpreted as a journey, a pilgrimage in search of an adequate frame of reference, meaning, value, purpose. But if it is only a quest without resolution, as Albert Camus dramatically suggests, one should seriously consider suicide, indicating thereby his conviction that a life without meaning or value or purpose is not worth living.

I was born in a maverick German-American family which had converted to Methodism. All my other relatives were solid Missouri Synod Lutherans, as befitted those of German heritage living in America. My father alone changed his name from Schmidt to Smith, and in a further token of disaffection or greater Americanism, converted from Lutheranism to Methodism. As a result, my early education was in the public schools rather than in the strongly disciplined and authoritarian Lutheran parochial system.

In retrospect, I cannot really say I regret my Methodist upbringing. It gave me something to react against, to sharpen my teeth on, and it familiarized me with religious ideas, which I took, even then, very seriously.

Our Methodist church in Fort Wayne, Indiana, was conservative, not fundamentalist. That is to say, there was some leeway for challenges and interpretations. There was no rigid, hidebound, unchallengeable dogmatism. I recall friendly discussions in which questions were raised. If everything on earth is placed here by God solely for man, as Genesis clearly states, then where do insects, mosquitoes, snakes, and germs fit in? And if only Adam and Eve were our progenitors, then where did Cain and Abel find their wives?

Even as a small child I loved ideas, I loved to debate, and the Epworth League youth group and the Sunday School classes were my forums. I must have been a real trial to my teachers, for I was willing to accept nothing on their authority alone. I wanted to think everything through for myself. By the time I was eleven or twelve I had concluded that the stories of the miracles were plain silly. And did not this God, Jahweh, of the Old Testament seem much like a crotchety old man? Unbelievable! And I told my Sunday School teacher so. There must be a Creativity factor, however, and if there is a God then He must be something impersonal, something on the order of a giant energy force like lightning.

Mind you, I was not giving up God, just the Bible version, which struck me as childish and simple-minded. Thus my quest for God continued to fascinate and agitate me. What was the answer? I found it terribly important to resolve this problem. When I was a freshman in high school I conducted my own test. If my belief was important to me, ought it not be important to God? I would let Him intervene directly and provide my answer. I lay on my bed looking out the window one evening and challenged God. If He wanted me to believe in Him, he must flash a light in the sky during the next five minutes. Breathlessly I awaited in expectation. The seconds and the minutes ticked away. Finally, just as I was about to give up, a distinct light appeared in the sky, remained for an instant, then faded away. I was really stupefied. All this just for me! But then the truth flooded in upon me. What I had seen was a falling star, a meteor. But still it was an enigmatic, baffling experience, for if God were to answer my challenge, how else would he set a light in the sky for me?

Evidently I was never really a truly committed Methodist, for I was always searching. I toyed with Rosicrucianism. I was enamored breifly with Roman Catholicism — an organization which claimed to have *all* the answers, which was perfectly and absolutely authoritarian. It was worth investigating, I thought. I attended a number of Masses, read its literature. And it was true; here was an institution which had an answer for everything! But, alas! they were not answers I found satisfying and beyond criticism. It was the same problem I had had with my Methodist Sunday School teachers: I had to be satisfied in my own mind; the answer had to meet my own standard of truth.

In time I discovered I was a natural-born iconoclast. I loved to pull down Establishment arguments. By now I was reading widely and I was delighted to find the fields of literature and philosophy filled with these wonderful iconoclasts, critics of the status quo, image breakers. I made my discovery of H. L. Mencken, Bernard Shaw, Voltaire, Arthur Schopenhauer and his *Essays in Pessimism*, and dear, overwhelming Bertrand Russell. Harry Elmer Barnes, the sociologist and social philosopher, opened my eyes to the irrationalities and injustices of the social system. I listened to Norman Thomas and came to worship him.

I am sorry to confess it, but during this period of my life I came to enjoy being in opposition to just about anything. I was a rebel; tearing things down seemed to satisfy my needs. And a rebel I was when I went to Wittenberg College, with its required classes in religion. I set out to become a thorn in the flesh of Dr. Paul Heisey, head of the religion department. Fortunately for me he was old and mellow and impressed by anyone so interested in his subject as to be willing to take him on in class. He proved a friendly opponent. He even loaned me a review copy of a new book by the University of Chicago humanist, E. A. Burtt. For the first time I became aware of humanism as a movement. Indeed, it was a respectable position taken by many topflight philosophical and academic minds. It even published a magazine, *The Humanist*.

In a "come-outer" group, like the Unitarian Church or Ethical movement, it is easy at first to be an "aginner," to have deadly hostility for anything that reminds one of one's unemancipated past. One is still struggling to free oneself. Negativism, however, though satisfying for awhile, eventually becomes a poor diet. And yet the fever must run its course. As Albert Camus has said, "Nihilism must be experienced in its fulness before a positive position is reached."

By the time I began study for the Unitarian ministry at the Federated Theological Faculty of the University of Chicago, I was looking for an effective articulation of a positive naturalistic and humanistic philosophy of religion. At the time, existentialism was a fashionable campus topic, though few seemed to have read the primary sources. One professor, Dr. James Luther Adams, was sympathetic but was not an active missionary. Mostly I saw existentialism in a context of pessimism and despair, as something in close rapport with the gloomy atmosphere in Europe immediately following World War II. Hence I continued for some time to see it as the enemy of healthy humanism. Even a seminar on Kierkegaard cleared nothing up. The Dane *was* gloomy and I was not prepared for his drastic rejection of reason and his equally fervent advocacy of faith and feeling alone. "Subjectivity is truth," said Soren Kierkegaard.

I was still too much the rationalist to understand what he was talking about. Reason still had my full confidence and I thought of mysteries only as areas not yet cleared up by science and reason. Indeed, I was not too far from "Scientism" — a belief that science is the be-all and end-all, the ultimate judge and answer to all things, even ethics and values and morals and the good life.

It is said sometimes that an existentialist is a disappointed rationalist. The more I got into theology and philosophy, the more I became aware that there are no final answers. Even my idolized Bertrand Russell, after a lifetime of effort, was compelled to admit the impossibility of establishing absolutely reliable knowledge. It seems that logic and science are just not very helpful when it comes to ethics, morals, or social philosophy: e.g., it is impossible solely by reason or science to prove it is bad to enjoy inflicting pain. For science cannot deal with ultimate meanings. I came to see that a purely rationalistic humanism was shallow and inadequate. For me humanism had to be made existential.

In order to explain my conversion to existential humanism it might be appropriate to sketch in just a few of the rudimentary ideas, inasmuch as "existentialism" is likely the most distorted and misunderstood term in the entire field of ideas. There is an explanation for this. By its very nature it objects strenuously to definitions, systems, and creeds, and hence resists being enclosed or labeled. Existentialists are individualists par excellence. Perhaps the best one can do in response to the constant request for a definition is to deal with certain themes, motifs, and characteristic ideas.

Jean-Paul Sartre's wrote that "existence precedes essence." Implicit here is the notion that one's being, one's sense of self, the whole subjective side of life, must always have top priority significance. Reason, thought, the whole realm of abstract conceptual

131

thinking, come later and must not serve as *the* guide or definition of our true being.

In existentialism there is always the stress on the interior mind, the immediacy of the present, the uniqueness of the subjective, the centrality of personal involvement and commitment. In the beginning was Being. Freud might be cited in confirmation: he maintained that reason is not prior or even absolute. First is the unconscious. Primordial being is the beginning, to be sure, but then comes reason, much later — in fact very much later — as a development. And reason, in Freudian terms, is but a tool, a mechanism for inventing rationalizations or excuses for what the unconscious desires.

Vital consequences flow from this stress on subjectivism as setting forth one's ultimate relation to truth. It suggests that reason and logic cannot touch upon the ultimate problems of the human condition. Could it be that the idea of "objective truth" is a middle-class, bourgeois concept? And, again, if it follows that life is basically "absurd" — that is, defying rational explanation — then how can there be an objective meaning to it? May not the purpose of life be to enjoy and savor its many possibilities? *May not the meaning of life simply be the unfolding of it?*

Let me be very explicit about my conviction that existentialism does not replace or nullify my basic humanism. Rather, for me, it is an added ingredient, something that makes for a richer mixture. And, insofar as Ethical humanism is an open-minded and open-ended position, it can gain, not lose, from a deeper philosophical grounding which makes for a greater sophistication and emotional and experiential worth. Existentialism is a method of correcting certain unnecessary distortions in an overly scientific form of humanism — a form with an overweening concern with technology, submission to a passe rationalism, and a still continuing addiction to utopian expectations based on naive notions of human nature.

To my mind humanism and existentialism are fully compatible. It is disappointing to me that I have been able to stake out my claim to existential humanism with so little competition from colleagues in the Ethical movement. Some years ago a prominent Leader was most hostile to my interest and tended to see me as a heretic. Another, a well-known professor of philosophy, chided me with Olympian pronouncements that existentialism was passe, merely a temporary fad, and would soon be dead! At the time, some seventeen years ago, I had just completed special studies with New York University's Professor William Barrett, of *Irrational Man* fame, and was working up some courses to teach in adult night schools. A tiny

132

handful of universities included existentialism as a subject of study. Today hundreds of schools feature the subject, and hundreds of volumes have come off the presses in continuing tribute to popular interest.

It is a widely recognized fact that existentialism is the only philosophy today that speaks to people and thus has a public base of support. Conventional academic philosophy long ago eliminated itself from public interest by its specialized concern with linguistics and logical positivism, regarded by non-philosophers as dull and sterile. It is no coincidence that the most honored and highly regarded philosophers of our time are existentialist: Martin Heidegger, Karl Jaspers, Martin Buber, Albert Camus, Jean-Paul Sartre, Paul Tillich, and so on. I would challenge anyone to come up with an equally prestigious list of non-existentialists! Accordingly, the influence of existentialism is pervasive in our culture. Art, literature, poetry, drama, politics, developments in the counter-culture: all in their present manifestations can only be understood and appreciated in this context.

The abdication of formal, academic philosophy, along with the perfect symmetry of existentialism with the cultural and intellectual temper of our time, suggests an obvious conclusion. Ethical Culture cannot afford to identify itself as a dry, rationalistic, secular religion. Indeed it is suicidal to do so. Rather it is apparent that the rich insights of existentialism into the emotional, non-rational, Dionysian aspects of human nature can make our humanism not only viable but the most accurate answer to human needs. Indeed, realism demands it! Whether we can distinguish between what human nature actually is and what we *naively think it ought to be* is crucial to our survival. And as the only religious group completely committed to humanism, Ethical Culture will at its peril reject that excellent advice of the ancient Roman playwright, Terence: "Nothing human is alien to me."

Fortunately, the Ethical movement's founder, Felix Adler, was a realist. It is thus hardly a coincidence that his mentor and the greatest influence upon his early formulation of Ethical Culture was Immanuel Kant, the father of pragmatism and existentialism. It was Kant who demonstrated that there are inelectable limits to reason, and reason is therefore unable to deal with the heart of reality. Human beings can know the world only in the limited ways translated by our senses. In destroying the claims of rationalism, Kant prepared the foundations of modern existentialism, which holds to the priority of existence, experience, and feeling.

We are now brought full circle. Kant was Felix Adler's mentor, and here we find the inevitable tie-in between the Ethical movement and existentialism. Adler, as a Kantian, was compelled to admit that reason is of little assistance in providing ethical sanctions. The answer cannot come from without, through the imposition of science and logic. The only answer comes from within. Ethics is existential; its sources derive from an inner moral sense of obligation and duty. A good act, therefore, is that which is done from a sense of duty.

Ethics is always deeply personal; it is not an abstraction. Nor should it be the subject of detached speculation, but of deep and passionate involvement, in the same sense that my own existence is a passionate reality to me and not a mere abstract concept to theorize about.

TOWARD A HUMANISTIC PIETISM:
COMING DOWN TO WHERE I OUGHT TO BE

Michael S. Franch

PEOPLE COME to Ethical Culture from many backgrounds; it is one of the causes of the great richness of the Ethical movement and one of its great strengths. We are, by and large, a movement of "come-outers" from other denominations. For some people, joining an Ethical Society represents a glad rejection of a former association, an easy shifting of denominational labels. Others are still working out their relationship with their past even after joining; for them belonging to an Ethical Society represents a shift of identity painfully accomplished.

People come to Ethical Culture in many ways. Some drift into the movement, joining a Society in the casual way that one might join any other voluntary association in which one feels comfortable. For others, membership means a change in the sense of personal identification — the "who am I?" Some people discover us and affiliate with all the emotion of a conversion experience; how common is the exclamation, "Where have you been all my life? I've been looking for something like Ethical Culture for years!" Others, in another form of the conversion experience, resist joining, wrestle with themselves (often for years), and participate without officially joining before finally submitting a membership application.

I count myself as one for whom joining was the result of a slow working out of my relationship to my past, as one who took a long time to decide but who, once decided, found that the decision meant not only a change in religious identity but in how I live my life.

I had known of Ethical Culture but had no contact with it before meeting and marrying Eileen. The first Ethical Culture ceremony I attended was my own wedding, performed by Edward Ericson in the Washington Society building in August 1967. Through Eileen's involvement I too became involved in the activities of the Washington Society, but as an active non-member friend rather than as a member. I was just a fellow traveler until I joined the Baltimore Society in 1975.

Although long adrift from participation in my ancestral religion, a sense of identity, a feeling of being part of a heritage, a fear of betrayal of a long tradition kept me from joining the Ethical movement. The sense of religion, of tradition, of peoplehood held me even though I had for years been outside the formal religion of Judaism as well as outside the Jewish community — and Judaism, perhaps more than other religions, is a religion of community. For years I could not formally remove myself from that community of heritage and peoplehood; I could not formally change my religious sense of self — in short, could not apostatize, could not say, "I am no longer a Jew, I am an Ethical Culturist." It was not until I could finally sort out my feelings about where I really belonged that I could come forward and say, "This is where I belong and want to be. This is who I am."

It was not a question of rejecting the idea of a diety. I have never been much concerned with the "God Question." On joining the Baltimore Society I described myself as a theist, but noted that I was essentially a "believing agnostic (for which I was taken to task, lovingly I hope, by one of the members for the contradiction of claiming to both believe and say I didn't know). When I was twenty I could truthfully tell my Selective Service Board, in applying for conscientious objector status, that I believed in a Supreme Being, although I defined my obligation to that Supreme Being in strictly humanistic terms. I do not know whether there is a God or whether there is not, and the question does not concern me; I believed when I was twenty that the only way to serve God was through humanity, and sixteen years later, although I have no compunction in describing myself simply as an agnostic humanist, the essential thrust of my answer remains the same. Questions about the existence or nonexistence of a diety concern me not at all; questions of human behavior are to me central.

Indeed, if it were the God Question that was central to my religious dilemma, I probably could have resolved it sooner than I did. The theist moving to atheism reduces what has been abandoned into nothingness (although all too often the principle of negation becomes the new god and God takes on more life denied than affirmed). Since the concept has meaning only if believed, ceasing to believe it destroys it and its power. But severing a sense of identification with people does not evaporate the people or the past. I am sure that many former Methodists, for example, always carry with them something of the warmth of Methodist fellowship; I know many former Catholics who have never been able to escape the well-wrought ties of community and doctrine. This affectional tie to past affiliation is especially true when that which is left is left not so much out of rejection of something as generically bad but out of one's personal development ("It may be okay for others, but it's not for me"). There is, certainly, much of contemporary American Jewish life that I reject, to say nothing of the concept of religion as centered on a specific people — but I cannot anathematize it. Unlike others who left their religions of birth or choice and who bear the burden of the bad things their religion did to them — inculcating guilt or building narrow prejudices that it may take a lifetime to work out — I left with kind though ambivalent feelings. I wish those Jews well who seek to further the ethical thrust of Jewish life and to liberate American Judaism from its materialist cage; they have a noble task, but it is not my task.

I have my past, and like any past it is both a burden of continually resolving ambivalences and a thank-offering for helping to make me what I am. It gave me part of my sense of justice and outrage at injustice; it gave me a sense of continuity in human history; it told me that there can be joy and warmth in religion; and it taught me that there can be value and community outside the stream of belief shared by the majority around me.

I was reared in a small midwestern city of about 50,000 people. There was a small Jewish community of about 200 families that had organized, in my grandfather's day, to support a synagogue. It was a Conservative synagogue as the middle-way compromise, but the Orthodox held their own early Friday-evening and Saturday-morning services. I received the usual, rather minimal, Jewish education: Hebrew school two or three days a week after regular school, Sunday School, private lessons with the rabbi to prepare me for my bar mitzvah (I typed this essay on my bar mitzvah typewriter) and confirmation, after which I graduated from the Sunday School into the B'nai B'rith Sunday morning bowling league. Our household was not particularly observant — we did not keep kosher — but my mother did light the Friday-night candles and I chanted the blessing over the wine.

In my teens I attended Jewish camps for two or three summers. I was not particularly learned in Judaism but I did develop a strong feeling of Jewish identity — a sense of being part of a tradition, of having a heritage written in the blood of martyrs, of being, in a certain fortunate way, outside the mainstream of American and European religious tradition. I felt a strong obligation not to betray Judaism's history, not to step outside that stream of humanity that for two thousand years had kept the flame alive through almost constant persecution.

This is not to say that I had no "religious" feeling or was unmoved by certain pietistic urges. I still remember with affection the brief period in my youth when I attended the Orthodox Saturday-morning services with "the regulars" in my hometown synagogue. And at the conclusion of those services there were refreshments in the basement social hall: delicious egg cookies, cake, and a shot of whiskey. Let the record show that I probably had my first drink in the YMHA Temple in Aurora, Illinois.

I did not long attend those services, however, although for reasons having more to do with youthful desires to spend Saturday mornings in other ways than to theological misgivings. For some years, even into college and graduate school, I attended High Holiday services, although irregularly and with increasing discomfort. And so I began to drift away from Judaism and toward Ethical Culture.

Among the values I brought with me to Ethical Culture were a generalized humanism, social concern, and a belief in individual worth and uniqueness. These, certainly, are among the key principles of Ethical Culture, and among the reasons I was attracted to it. I was also involved in the civil rights movement, and I welcomed an organization that not only was committed to equality philosophically but that *practiced* it. I was impressed with the outward manifestation of inner commitment.

If, then, my values were already formed, and if I already felt myself part of the larger, small-"e" ethical community, and if I had a sense of tension about leaving my religious past and my relationship to it, why did I finally join the Ethical movement?

Because I liked the warmth and sense of community of a particular Ethical Society. But also — and this, I should say in all honesty, became clearer in retrospect — because I realized that generalized commitment is generally a socially (and often personally) worthless commitment. For our commitments, our values, our ideals to have meaning and life, they must be expressed. Without a concrete manifestation of them they are disembodied — not only socially useless but often personally unformed.

Perhaps it is my Old Testament background that makes me particularly fond of David Saville Muzzey's definition of an Ethical Society. Muzzey, who himself came out of New England Congregationalism, described an Ethical Society as composed of "mutually stimulating seekers after righteousness." I don't claim to be righteous, but I do claim to be seeking to be righteous.

The pursuit of righteousness, unfortunately, has an old-fashioned sound to today's ears and even seems self-righteous and stiff-necked. It conjures up, perhaps, images of dogmatic religion that many members wished to leave behind them when they joined the Ethical movement. I am sorry if that is so, for I think it is wrong, and the wrong image for the movement. It does not, I admit, convey the joy of membership, the pleasure I feel when joining with men and women of various religious backgrounds and races in a mutual quest, people who feel as I do, who are as I am, who seek to be as I seek to be. This is more than the clan feeling of race or ethnicity. It is the solidarity of those who *have* chosen as opposed to those who feel they *were* chosen.

The great transforming event (if event is not understood as a single, overwhelming, dramatic moment) that was my "conversion experience" was the awareness that by affiliating with an Ethical Society — by taking Ethical Culture as my religion — I would not change my sense of the past from which I grew nor would I diminish my non-participation in the ongoing Jewish community life, but that it would place me formally where I already was.

Because my own religious development has not been marked by sharp divides and tormenting inner struggles, because I was not so intensely involved with Jewish religious, communal, or intellectual life that my breaking away left a bitter wound, I left with feelings of affection and even of nostalgia, and certainly not with rancor.

Equally important, I left without opposition to religion in general. I knew the positive value of religion. I had good friends who were deeply motivated by their Christianity; their Christianity was and never could be mine, but I was moved by the outward manifestation of their belief — their commitment, their spirituality, their humanity — that grew from, or at least was nurtured by, their particular belief. I know that believers in particular religions have been guilty of terrible atrocities, atrocities fueled by their faith and done in its name. I also know that religious belief has been a great force for liberation and love, for justice and freedom.

Because I am in the "religious wing" of the Ethical movement, because I came to Ethical Culture without the burden of anti-religious hostility that many of our members carry, I see much of value in the traditional religious terminology, although defined humanistically, of course. Terms such as holiness or sanctity still have meaning to me — not other-worldly, heavenly meanings, but this-worldly, human meanings for here and now.

And so, because I see myself in the tradition of the religious, I am drawn to religious models. I am impressed by the quality of inner life and the engagement with the outer world of many believers of traditional faiths. While I do not share their specific formulations of faith, I would be happy to integrate their sense of the wholeness of life into my own humanistic way of life. The term that best expresses what I seek is "humanistic pietism."

Pietism requires more definition, and my coupling of the two terms may seem somewhat paradoxical. Pietism can best be described as a religion of the heart rather than the head, of direct religious feeling over the intellect. In the Christian context it is usually used to describe a movement that began in seventeenth-century Germany. Within Judaism the Hassidic rejection of rabbinic scholasticism in the eighteenth century was a manifestation of pietism; indeed, "hassid" means "pious one." Pietism is in stark contrast to the religion of the Enlightenment which, especially in its deistic form, emphasized rationality and the intellect and deprecated emotion or "enthusiasm."

We in the Ethical movement are heirs to the Enlightenment, and it is a proud heritage. I too count myself in the Enlightenment tradition. I too highly value intellectuality, openness, a willingness to test one's beliefs rationally; I too abhor dogmatism. It must be understood that when I talk of humanistic pietism I am not talking about anti-intellectualism or unbridled emotionalism. It is the compassion, not the irrationalism, that I draw from pietism. If this pietism puts me on the religious "right" of the Ethical movement, it is still within the context of my position on the "left" of the American religious landscape and I am sure a traditional pietist would disown me as hopelessly cerebral as well as theologically wrong-headed.

Religion is an affair of the heart as well as the head, and without the engine of the heart we become, as Ethical Culturists, the anti-thesis of our vaunted "deed before creed" — we become a religion of profession ("I believe") rather than of action ("I do"), and even less will we have a religion that defines our being ("I am"); our benevolence and social activism becomes abstract and institutional rather than personal and concrete, becomes cause-oriented rather than people-oriented, and manifests itself toward groups and not toward the human reality of the group. We lose the passion for engagement with the injustices of life and the sense of personal obligation that the young Felix Adler and his followers felt in looking at the plight of the industrial worker and the moral chaos of their day. We lose the sense that humanistic engagement with life is not just cause- or reform-oriented but the daily expression of our humanism in all our relationships.

We need both detachment and engagement, both reason and compassion. We need the essential ability to step outside ourselves and to look within ourselves. We must be analytic, we must be rational, we must avoid rigidity and fanaticism by the cool use of our intellect. And we must leave room for *feeling;* we must risk having "our heart go out" to others; we must risk — as did the early Quakers and Methodists, as did observant Jews through history, as did the reformers of countless religions — the ridicule and snide remarks of others and even our own doubts to live our lives in the light of our faith. We must be pious; we must live up to the commandments of our religion. They are not commandments handed down from on high; they are the commandments of our hearts. As we have a personal religion, so we are called to a personal holiness.

It is a humanistic holiness that I seek, and I have found my way to seek it through the Ethical movement. I have come down to where I ought to be.

SOLUTIONS FOR A WORLD GROWN SMALLER?

Joseph Chuman

I JOINED the Leadership Training Program at the New York Society for Ethical Culture in November of 1969 at the age of 21, shortly after receiving a bachelor's degree in Classical Greek and Latin. This choice was made at a critical time in my life, in that I married a strong desire to express myself to others with a sense of ethical idealism which had been greatly animated by my resistance to the Vietnam War.

I trust that the decision to skip an academic career for one which encompasses a wider range of human experience, as does Ethical Leadership, was not solely a product of reason and thought. For our choices, no matter how greatly pondered, in the final analysis must still satisfy deeply-felt longings which often govern our thoughts themselves. In Ethical Culture I have found a milieu which both intellectually makes sense and has fulfilled my deeper needs for emotional growth and social interaction.

Prior to my college years my intellectual pursuits centered around the accumulation of facts about nature and the world. In short, I had an insatiable curiosity which compelled me to become a great memorizer of all sorts of disassociated facts. It was not until I entered college and took an introductory course in philosophy that the importance of how facts relate to one another caught my interest. In other words, the realm of ideas opened up to me. I can well recall the moment this occurred. The instructor was elucidating to our class of freshmen the passage in Plato in which he outlines his theory of Ideal Forms and how they press themselves upon our consciousness so as to engender thoughts and concepts. It's as if our minds were to intuit the essential quality of things which leave imprints within our brains as ideas. The thought of the presence of ideas all around us, the interrelationship among them, and the fact that they might have a dynamic influence on our lives profoundly caught my imagination and shaped my intellectual directions for the next several years. Whether the Platonic theory of Forms was an accurate conception of reality or existed only in Plato's mind made no difference to me. The door to the intellectual process had been opened for me and a new world presented itself.

The emergence of my own late adolescence, coupled with very serious stresses in my family life (my mother died when I was twelve; my father was a partial invalid toward the end of his life) led me to the realization of realms of experience beyond the purely intellectual. In the search for a significant, gratifying life, what becomes essential is not only what one *thinks* about the nature of things, but how one *feels* about one's self and others. In addition to the world of objective truth, one must find a subjective truth — a truth of feeling as well as of thought. It was with the unraveling of this discovery that I came to the personal conviction that the only valid existence is a social existence. It was this realization that gave body and substance to a nascent humanist outlook, just as my intellectual pursuits gave it direction. This is not to say that I had not previously been aware of emotional feelings and preferences, but rather it was during the period of my late teens and early twenties that the significance of psychological integration and the integration of thought and feeling for me arose as a matter of great personal importance. It was at this point, toward the end of my undergraduate work, that the development of my own character became a self-conscious activity. It was also at this time that I joined the Ethical movement.

The successive stages of my philosophical development at all times have mirrored my understanding of the Ethical movement, so that in great measure that understanding and my personal view have coincided. It is one of our philosophy's great strengths that it is not a static phenomenon but an ever-evolving body of ideas, yet one anchored securely in our real experience, both individual and collective. In a deeper sense, Ethical Culture as a philosophy is our experience thrust before us in ideational form, tempered by reason and sustained by compassion and faith in human nature. Our experience, once so expressed, serves as a finger pointing the way for future action and growth. As Felix Adler once tersely stated, "Our inspiration comes not from above but from ahead."

But if Ethical Culture is a vital and fertile milieu which leads to expansion and refinement of our moral stature, then we have to state not only what we believe but *how* we believe it. To affirm what we believe need not suggest that the thing believed has any consequence to our lives. It can exist as an idea fundamentally isolated from our conduct and character. The exposition of *how* we hold a set of beliefs reveals that we are in a position of active relationship to them, that they bear a dynamic effect on our lives.

In my initial phases I primarily assumed an existential interpretation of Ethical Culture which appreciated above all its view of the development of the individual, believing that the psychological emancipation of each would be the precondition for the happiness of all. My individualistically oriented humanism emanated not only from a passionate concern for individual liberties and rights but also from my direct observations of the conflicts in people's lives which led to their continuing unhappiness. In simplest terms, I felt the key to social amelioration was to be found in overcoming those psychological forces which impede individual growth, in that society can be viewed as a conglomerate of individuals and perhaps little beyond that.

True enough, personal growth does involve an ongoing relationship amongst family and friends and with those who otherwise touch our lives, and in this sense personal freedom and well-being cannot stand apart from a social interaction. Yet a theory of human happiness which sees individual psychology as *the* exclusive point of departure is not equitable with a complete humanism. Taking a broad view, this has been the general assumption and modus operandi of the traditional religions: of Buddhism with its emphasis on the individual search for Nirvana, of Christianity with its doctrine of personal salvation, and of Judaism, though to a far lesser extent.

Our contemporary humanism must become increasingly aware of the social determinants which make for ethical personality — the cultural, the economic, the political. Idealistic appeals to individual excellence should continue unabated, but in isolation from social concern and analysis they leave us philosophically anachronistic and at worst piously self-indulgent.

In this regard I am no longer a staunch advocate of existentialism and certainly not a believer in radical freedom. It seems apparent to me that there are real forces, the biological and economic as well as the social, which are beyond the grasp of our responsibility and our reasonable control, yet how we relate to the uncontrollable can make all the difference in the world.

A complete humanism needs to include such concerns within its compass. More specifically, as it addresses social problems it should more deeply consider the two most significant dynamic theories of human social evolution of our age, Marxism and Freudianism, particularly the ways in which they complement one another. Neither one can serve as a basis for humanism alone or even together. Marxism, on the one hand, has never developed an adequate philosophy of individual behavior. While Freudianism, on the other hand, lacks an appreciation for the possibility of radical cultural and social change and determinants of that change beyond the interaction of family members.

If we are humanists, then we must take the establishment of equality seriously, and this to my mind necessitates economic equality also. A humanistic socialism, in my view, is the only major philosophic and political movement which gives the obliteration of excessive economic disparity its just due. Yet at the same time we must be wary of not summarizing all individual hardship and oppression under the umbrella of economic cure. The mind, as Freud has analyzed better than anyone, operates from determinants which are just minimally related to the economic sphere. Man indeed is a social and economic being, but a biological one also, who at least for the time being is reared in families and greatly molded by them. One of the most challenging and fruitful questions of our times is how greatly the individual psychology of Freud can be harmonized with the social philosophy of Marx. Neither, as mentioned, can serve as the "official" philosophy behind Ethical Culture, but both, as methods of criticism and as vehicles for interpreting the social realm, are indispensible for the humanist.

My shift in emphasis from an Ethical Culture which is individualistically oriented to one which appreciates the broader social dimension most probably reflected a subtle rearrangement of my own psychic economy. In overcoming many of the internal conflicts of my earlier days, I was prepared to approach more wholeheartedly the world of external reality. In general, I have always been fascinated by the relationship between the psychological and the material, the subjective and objective. This appreciation of itself gives rise to the dimension of experience I term spiritual.

Since the use of the term *spiritual* is controversial within our movement, I think it bears some explanation. In the strict sense, I consider myself a naturalist and a materialist. I see no evidence of disembodied spirits or deities, and find the concept aesthetically complicating and cumbersome. Our mind, our thoughts, our feelings, our sense of reality, and even our subtlest intuitions are all in the last analysis reduceable to causes to be found in our natural and material make-up. Although the materialist view, I feel, is correct, it is something we all resist because it seems to make life too mechanical and too determined. Yet it's from this very resistance that our sense of self and autonomy is born. And it is imperative that we respect this autonomy and nurture it; it is this realm of the subjective and the autonomous that defines our humanity and our sanity. To carry it one step further, the presence of the subjective in all of us is itself an objective characteristic of our humanity. This subjective impulse tempered by the conditions of the real world gives rise to our culture, our religion, our science, and our ethics. It also gives rise to a spiritual sense.

By the spiritual, I connote that ineffable understanding that there is unity in nature, and unity between man and nature and between man and man. It can be wonderment at the cyclical patterns of nature and reflection of our place in that scheme. It can be the reverence that a mother feels when contemplating how she with her newborn child are living a human experience had by mothers and children for millenia in the past and for eons into the future. The spiritual can be found in the identification one has with great and inspirational ideas, or in poetry and music which moves us and resonates with significance that appears timeless. It can be felt in working in solidarity with others toward the goals of social justice or with just one friend when the walls of isolation crumble and we sense that we are one with another.

The subjective and spiritual, though ultimately and darkly anchored in our material natures, are not wispy or without force. In our imaginations and intellects we create visions of the future and chart the directions that we embark upon.

The genius of Ethical Culture is that it has been able to combine this respect for the spiritual and the human with the knowledge which modern science and inquiry have revealed to us. It has done this in the service of progress aimed at the ideal of a full life for all. In a world grown smaller, where the cries for justice, equality, and a sense of meaning in life have grown more strident, Ethical humanism may indeed be the religion of the future.

IN THE AGE OF SHADOWS, DOES LIBERAL RELIGION HAVE A FUTURE?

Joseph L. Blau

ANNIVERSARIES ARE milestones, especially when one is young. They mark off stages of growth, both physical and mental. They symbolize, or seem to, an increase in understanding. They provide occasions for both retrospect and prospect. At the time of an anniversary, it is characteristic of humans — who might be defined as organic beings with a sense of time, or even as the inventors of the past — to look back on their lives since the last milestone, the last significant anniversary, and to estimate with satisfaction or dissatisfaction what they have done in the interval. It is equally characteristic of humans — who might also be defined as organic beings with a sense of purpose, or even as the inventors of the future — to project their thought toward the next milestone, and the next, and the next . . . .

Anniversaries can also be millstones, especially as one grows older. They mark off the stages of decline, both physical and mental. They symbolize, or seem to, a decrease in vital force, in creativity, an entropic aversion to change or novelty, a withdrawing from the future and its hopes into the past and its memories. It may well be that the most characteristically human verse in the Old Testament is to be found in the sixth chapter of the book of Genesis: "There were giants in the earth in those days." To dwell on the past is to attempt to live off the past, to borrow from *then* a life that we no longer

147

have *now*. Both biologically and psychologically, it is an understandable "ploy" to conceal, even from ourselves, our increasing asthenia, our growing debilitation, the sclerotic processes of our own aging.

Human institutions, too, even as human persons, have histories; they come into being, flourish, decay, and pass away. They are the creatures of humanity's senses of time and purpose. Institutions are temporal incarnations of human purposes, embodiments of human ideals and goals. They are ineluctably intentional; persons may come into existence as the consequence of the chance meeting of *this* particular spermatozoon and *that* particular egg, but institutions can be born only deliberately.

Because they have histories, human institutions have anniversaries. There are significant dates in the lives of institutions, times for the backward look and the forward look; there are times for evaluation of what has been done toward the achievement of the stated goals of the past, but also for the assessment of the adequacy of the current interpretation of the goals and purposes of the institution; there are times, too, for taking a fresh look at the validity of the goals themselves. To fail to use the occasion for self-congratulation would be inhuman; to use it only for self-congratulation would turn the milestone into a millstone by subordinating the needs of the future to the pieties of the past.

The question is inevitable: What would the founders think of us and of what we have done with the heritage they bequeathed to us? Another question is more important and less often asked: What will our descendants think of us and of the heritage we bequeath to them? An institution composed exclusively of descendants is moribund; live institutions are made up of ancestors and descendants.

The Ethical movement has attained to a major anniversary. Founded in 1876, barely beyond the memory span of some persons still alive today, it not long ago reached the century mark. The anniversary provided the occasion for proclaiming the great achievements of the first hundred years. This represents what I might be tempted to call the "Lot's wife syndrome," the compulsive backward look that turned the lady, according to the biblical legend, into a pillar of salt. The vitality and the living force of any movement, however, is reflected in what it sees as its *unfinished* business, its role in the future, not in the records of its past.

The same is true, too, in a smaller way of any significant anniversary of one segment of the Ethical movement. The intimate

148

recollections of the cozy beginnings of a Society, in this living room or that, the detailing of the intricacies of interpersonal relations within the group as it grew in size, the larger-than-life heroics of some of those who helped, the therapeutically deft wit of others who prevented possibly disastrous confrontations, the struggles for prestige and power endemic in organizational life — all this is history. And history can easily become filio-pietism; "there were," indeed, "giants in the earth in those days," we are tempted to say as we snuggle comfortably down into a nest created by *their* energetic pursuit of *their* dreams and *their* ideals and *their* visions, based on the needs of *their* situation.

There is nothing inherently wrong — or right, for that matter — in being an heir. We are all heirs to the extent that we inherit our genetic constitution; we are all heirs, in a larger and more impersonal sense, because we inherit and benefit from the collective achievements of humanity from time immemorial. What is wrong is to be nothing but heirs, to live our whole lives on the heritage of the past, to be consumers of the gains to humanity from the labors of our predecessors without restoring anything to the common stock or creating anything to replace what we have withdrawn. This is the ultimate prodigality, strip-mining the human spirit.

Apart from this general sense in which all people who now live are heirs of all people who have lived, those who have come together as Ethical humanists are among the constituents in the present of a liberating human tradition of great antiquity, the heirs of a long history of liberal, non-theistic religion. Even in the Old Testament, a major source-book of conventional theism as well as of fundamentalism, recent scholarship has identified a clearly humanist strain, especially in the book of Deuteronomy.

In the early days of the United States, Benjamin Franklin, John Adams, Thomas Jefferson, Thomas Paine, and many others sought to develop the outlines of a liberal religion for their age. But the nineteenth century witnessed the most significant flourishing of nontheistic religious movements in American life. It was, in large part, the revolt against the doctrinaire quality of conventional theism that led the New England Unitarians to transmute the traditional concept of the divine Christ to the concept of a human Jesus, a great moral teacher and leader rather than a supernatural saviour. William Ellery Channing, the most distinguished preacher in the early days of Unitarianism, said, "the adoration of goodness — this is religion." The transcendentalism of Emerson and Thoreau and the "manly theology" of Theodore Parker were humanistic, primarily concerned with man and his relation to his fellowman.

After the Civil War, non-theistic religious groups in the United States began to multiply. Unlike their pre-War precursors, which often attempted the establishment of Utopian communities, the newer groups continued to live in the world while attempting to change it by participating in social reform activities. Out of a split in the American Unitarian Association there began, in 1866, the important Free Religious Association, led for many years by Francis Ellingwood Abbott. At the founding meeting of the Free Religious Association, the sixty-three-year-old Ralph Waldo Emerson, already himself an institution in American life, was the first to enroll as a member. After much debate, the Association refused to make theism in any form a condition of membership and this enabled Felix Adler to join, to remain a member for ten years, to become president of the Association from 1878 to 1882 — that is, for several years after the foundation of the Society for Ethical Culture in New York City and of the Ethical movement.

The American Humanist Association, too, is descended from this same Free Religious Association, so the coming together of the American Ethical Union and the Humanist Association in the International Humanist and Ethical Union and in the sponsorship of *The Humanist* magazine is at least a partial re-joining of members of the same family. But the "family reunion" is incomplete. Rabbi Isaac Mayer Wise and other leading figures in American Reform Judaism were also members of the Free Religious Association, and, as I said before, so were many leaders of the more radical strains of Unitarianism. Moreover, Rabbi Mordecai M. Kaplan, the founder-leader of the Reconstructionist movement in contemporary Judaism, has defined his own position as humanistic and, many years ago, declared that Felix Adler was the most able of America's nineteenth-century Jewish thinkers, and that the inability of Judaism to retain Adler's allegiance was a measure of the weakness and limitations of the Jewish community. There is more to the family of liberal religion in America than merely humanists and Ethical Culturists, and far more to the historical genealogy of the Ethical movement than those who are members today. There is no doubt that liberal religion has a past, which is also the past of the Ethical movement.

We live, however, at a time when the tide seems to have turned against all types of liberalism, including liberal religion. We are informed on all sides and by almost all the agencies of communication in our society that liberalism is psychologically naive, that the day of liberalism is past, that the notion that people want to be masters of their own fate is a fossil survival of nineteenth-century ideas. The conservative mode of religious thought is extraordinarily prevalent in the United States today. Young people in the Christian tradition are submitting their minds to fundamentalist preachers. Among Roman Catholic Christians there are an increasing number of "traditionalist" groups — composed chiefly of the laity — who regard the post-Vatican II Church as having given up the true faith; they hold "underground" services in which the Mass is celebrated in Latin, as, obviously, God willed it to be celebrated. Many Jews of Reform background have turned back to the rigid orthodoxy of an earlier era or, alternatively, seek direction by joining Christian fringe groups like "Jews for Jesus." Some have become involved in ascetic or meditational groups formed on an Oriental, Buddhistic, or Hinduistic base.

There is a tremendous increase in many forms and varieties of occultism — not as a game, not for its "entertainment" values, like much of the spiritualism of the 1920s — but out of deep and sincere interest verging on, and in some cases passing over, into total belief. A few years ago I would have said that the increasing number of references to witches and witchcraft in the media were simply trendy and modish, and that they did not indicate any widespread pattern of belief in preternatural and transcendental phenomena. Today I could no longer dismiss the interest in occultism as frivolous. It is too widely manifested among leaders and potential leaders in American life. That *The Exorcist* was made into a movie and was, to quote *Newsweek*, "enthralling audiences across the country," is not what concerns me most. What concerns me is that actual exorcisms are being performed in our time and our country, under serious religious auspices. One such, that received much publicity, was performed in Daly City, California, by a Jesuit priest with the authorization from the archbishop of his diocese. The priest used the traditional Roman Catholic rite of exorcism, dating from the Middle Ages: "I cast you out, unclean spirits, along with every satanic power of the enemy, ever specter from Hell and all your fell companions." Let me report again in the words of *Newsweek:* "Assisted by as many as twenty lay helpers, he performed the ancient exorcism rite fourteen times in 29 days, burning incense in every room of the house and reciting prayers and chants." Because he was considered successful in exorcising the devil and his "fell companions" in this instance, he has since been called upon to perform other exorcisms which have not always been "successful."

From the point of view of a humanist, the claims that these and other incidents, movements, theories, and religions represent a birth of a new "consciousness," a "greening of America," are of interest only because they are so widely believed. The notion that we can move toward a new development of human consciousness by a retrogression into medieval modes of thinking is incredible. Even some advocates of the revised mysticism — or, perhaps, antimaterialisms — are aware of the possibility of a revived medievalism. Thus William Irwin Thompson, author of *At the Edge of History*, one of the most provocative — and provoking — books of the early 1970s, said, in an interview published in *Time* magazine: "We are again moving into a very hierarchical, mystical, Pythagorean, antidemocratic system. Half of me is in favor of that. The other half does not want to go through the Middle Ages all over again."

Even among those whom we have been accustomed to regard as close to our position, as our allies in liberalism and humanism, there are signs that point in the same direction. The renewed intensity with which the Reform Jews have begun to reconsider their relation to the idea of the commandments is symptomatic, as is the turn in the main-line Protestant churches away from humane and liberal to biblical and theological justifications of their social mission.

In such a world and in such a time, does liberal religion have a future? And if it does, what kind of future does it have? In the Ethical movement there are more Societies than there were half a century ago, but no more members; the overt humanist movement has always been tiny; Reform Judaism has not increased its membership significantly in the last twenty-five years, but Jewish orthodox synagogues have; main-line Protestantism has, if anything, lost ground to fundamentalism, pentacostalism, and other movements of the right; and there are only about one quarter of a million members in the merged Unitarian Universalist churches. Statistically, liberal religion today is an almost negligible element in American religious life.

Yet I am convinced that we should not despair — indeed that we may look forward with hope. I find history's long-range view a comfort and a solace. What is happening today has happened before and will probably happen again. It happened in the Mediterranean world — and especially in Greece — after the time of Alexander the Great. Gilbert Murray, one of the major classicists of the twentieth century, called the period "the Failure of Nerve." People had, so to speak, climbed out further and further on the branches of the tree of knowledge, especially in science and philosophy, but while this was happening the rude barbarians from Macedonia had destroyed the social and political basis of the stable world of the Greeks, the city-state. No longer seeing a role for themselves in the political world, the Greeks turned aside into the search for individual transcendental cults of salvation, but this did not last. Again when the stable administrative system of the Roman Empire lost vitality to the point where it was no longer able to repel the incursion of the barbarian tribesmen of Europe, an other-worldly turning was taken by the Romans — another "failure of nerve" that did not last.

The current "failure of nerve" will pass, too, in time. You and I may not live to see the turning of the tide of history. Historical trends have a notoriously long periodicity. Our children's children — or their children — may be the ones to witness the return from today's version of romantic supernaturalism to the sure knowledge that only by human hands working with human brains on the basis of the cumulated wisdom of humanity will genuine progress toward a humane world ever be made. That humane world to come will be egalitarian, libertarian, and fraternal — not "hierarchical . . . and antidemocratic." It will be a world at peace, not because cessation of hostilities is imposed upon belligerents by *force majeure*, but because reason has fully replaced unreason as the prevailing guide in human affairs. It will be — it must be — a world ruled by the democratic principle that the welfare of each person is the concern of all people, even as the welfare of all people is the concern of each person. It will be the world of which liberal religion has dreamed throughout the ages — but you and I will not live to see it come.

Our function — our role in the unending historical process of humanity seeking to humanize itself and thereby to humanize the world — is to keep the dream and the ideal alive in the minds of people until the present age of shadows has gone. We of the liberal religious movements are few and we are weak. We must learn together the meaning of commitment and mutual obligation, so that in spite of our small numbers and our lack of power we can continue to work toward the day of humankind that we envision.

Above all else, we must learn how to pass our vision on to our children and other young people, so that they, in their turn, may have the will to carry on further. For we do not know and cannot know how long it will be before the night of obscurantism is ended and the new day of humankind dawns. And we must not permit ourselves the luxury of a fragmented liberalism; we must not split with those who are on the same side for picayune and trivial reasons, for our history teaches us that this is the besetting sin of liberals. We must remember — and teach our children to remember — that, as Howard Nemerov once wrote, "The ideas one thinks of are of altogether less importance than the ideas one thinks with." The "ideas we think with" we share with our fellow liberals; we must not break with them because there are differences in "the ideas we think of."

It would be pretentious to say that the future lies entirely in our hands; we are too few for that. But we can at least serve to keep alive the gleam in an age of gloom.

NOTES ON CONTRIBUTORS

KHOREN ARISIAN, born in Boston in 1932, served as a Unitarian minister in Iowa and Florida and was active in civil rights work in the mid-1960s. He joined the Ethical movement in 1966 when he became Leader of the Boston Ethical Society. In 1968 he became a member of the Board of Leaders of the New York Society for Ethical Culture. He was among the founders of the Prison Reform Task Force of the New York Society and was instrumental in organizing the Ethical Culture School of Adult Education of which he was the director. He has served as president of the National Leaders' Council, is the author of more than sixty articles, and his first book, *The New Wedding*, was published by Alfred A. Knopf in 1973.

GEORGE E. BEAUCHAMP, born in Andrews, Indiana in 1906, has been dean of the National Leaders' Council since 1975. He served as Leader of the Washington Ethical Society from 1947 to 1957 and the Kissimmee (Florida) Ethical Fellowship from 1958 to 1964. He has also taught at Manchester College, Indiana, The Graduate School, Washington, D.C., and the University of South Florida.

ALGERNON D. BLACK, born in New York City in 1900, joined the New York Society for Ethical Culture as a staff member in 1923, was elected Leader in 1934, and has been Leader Emeritus of that Society since 1973. He taught in the Ethical Culture Schools for more than forty years and was chairman, Department of Ethics, 1943-1966. He founded the Encampment for Citizenship, the New York State Committee on Discrimination in Housing, and the National Committee Against Discrimination in Housing. He was appointed chairman of the Civilian Complaint Review Board of the Police Department of New York City. He is the author of five books and has recorded two records for children. He is the recipient of many citations and awards, including an honorary degree Doctor of Humane Letters, Long Island University, and Citation for Distinguished Citizenship and Exceptional Service from the City of New York.

JOSEPH L. BLAU, born in Brooklyn, New York, in 1909, is Professor Emeritus of Religion, Columbia University where he has taught since 1944. He is a widely published author in the fields of religion and philosophy. Among his publications are: *Modern Varieties of Judaism* and *Cornerstones of Religious Freedom in America.* He was one of the founding members of the Ethical Humanist Society of Long Island.

HOWARD BOX, born in New Jersey in 1926, was Leader of the Brooklyn Society for Ethical Culture from 1960 to 1976. Prior to joining the Ethical movement, he served as a Unitarian minister in Girard, Pennsylvania, Newburgh, New York, and Ottawa, Ontario. He maintained cordial ties with the Unitarian Universalist movement and the American Humanist Association throughout his stay in Brooklyn, and is again serving a Unitarian Church in Oak Ridge, Tennessee. He was among the founders of the Fellowship of Religious Humanists and his writings have appeared in their journal, *Religious Humanism.*

JOSEPH CHUMAN, born in New York City in 1948, is Leader of the Ethical Culture Society of Bergen County, New Jersey, which he joined in 1974 after serving two years as Leader of the Essex County Ethical Society in New Jersey. He has taught in the New York Public Schools and at Fieldston School. He founded the Northern New Jersey Chapter of Amnesty International in 1974 and has been its coordinator since then.

ARTHUR DOBRIN was born in Brooklyn, New York, in 1943. He has served as Leader of the Ethical Humanist Society of Long Island since 1968 prior to which he served, with his wife, as a Peace Corps Volunteer in Kenya, East Africa. For four summers he worked with the Encampment for Citizenship. He is the author of several books, including two books of poetry. He is the curator of the Center for Contemporary Long Island Poetry in Westbury, Long Island.

DALE H. DREWS, born in Kansas in 1935, is a social worker and therapist with Family Service of Burlington County, New Jersey, and is adjunct professor of sociology at Rutgers University. He served as Leader of the Queens Ethical Culture Society from 1964 to 1967.

MICHAEL ELDRIDGE, born in Oklahoma City in 1941, was director of the Baltimore Ethical Society, 1974-75, and assistant leader of the New York Society for Ethical Culture, 1975-77. He was ordained by the Disciples of Christ and served three Baltimore churches as pastor.

EDWARD L. ERICSON, born in Tampa, Florida in 1929, is currently Leader of the New York Society for Ethical Culture. Prior to joining the New York Society in 1971 he served as leader of the Washington Ethical Culture Society from 1959 to 1971. He also served as minister to Unitarian churches in Virginia and Oregon in the 1950s. He conceived and directed The Center for Applied Ethics and The Council on Educational Philosophy of the Ethical Culture Schools of New York. He was chairman of the Council for Humanist and Ethical Concerns. He has offered congressional testimony on such areas as civil rights, civil liberties, and selective service reform. He has contributed to numerous books and serves on the editorial board of *The Humanist.*

MICHAEL S. FRANCH, born in Aurora, Illinois in 1941, is acting leader of the Baltimore Ethical Society and editor of *ethical society: a magazine for ethical culture.* He has taught history at the University of Maryland, Morgan State University, and various Maryland community colleges. He was the coordinator of the First Conference on Baltimore History.

JAMES F. HORNBACK, born in Turney, Missouri in 1919, is leader of the Ethical Society of St. Louis. Before coming to

St. Louis in 1951 he served as leader of the Ethical Culture Society of Westchester for four years. He is a member of the National Board of the United Nations Association, Americans for Democratic Action, Americans United for Separation of Church and State, Planned Parenthood, and World Federalists. For six years he was chairman of the National Leaders' Council.

RICHARD KERN, born in Detroit, Michigan in 1932, is professor of history, Findlay College, and chairperson of its division of social science. He was part-time leader of the Cleveland Ethical Culture Society from 1975 to 1977. He is author of *John Winebrenner, 19th Century Reformer.*

JEAN SOMERVILLE KOTKIN, born in Montreal, Canada, is the executive director of the American Ethical Union.

PAUL R. MIGLIORE, born in 1944, was raised in Phoenix, Arizona, and Austin, Texas. He is associate leader of the New York Society for Ethical Culture. He is a member of the NGO delegation of International Humanist and Ethical Union at the United Nations and helped direct the Chilean Resettlement Project at the New York Society.

LESTER MONDALE, born nine miles from Walnut Grove, Minnesota in 1904, owns and manages an Ozark "Forest Crop" farm in Missouri. He has served in the liberal ministry since 1929, first as a Unitarian minister and then leader of the Philadelphia Ethical Culture Society from 1952 to 1959. In 1933 he was the youngest signer of the Humanist Manifesto. He has been president of the Fellowship of Religious Humanists, the Madison County (Missouri) Democratic Club, and is the author of seven books. He also served twice as a speech writer for his brother Walter's senatorial campaigns.

DONALD D. MONTAGNA, born in Springfield, Massachusetts in 1944, is Leader of the Washington Ethical Society.

CABLE NEUHAUS, editor of *A Lively Connection*, was born in 1947 in Munich, Germany. A free-lance writer and magazine correspondent, his articles and essays have appeared frequently in *The Humanist, People, Journal of Communication*, and *Pittsburgh Magazine*, as well as in a variety of other popular and scholarly periodicals. He has also written for *The Washington Post*, Random House publishers, and public television. Currently he is on leave of absence from the journalism faculty of Pennsylvania State University while working on a Doctor of Arts degree in English at Carnegie-Mellon University in Pittsburgh.

HOWARD B. RADEST, born in New York City in 1928, is co-chairman and secretary general of the International Humanist and Ethical Union and professor of philosophy, Ramapo College, New Jersey. He was executive director of the American Ethical Union, 1964-1970, and leader of the Ethical Culture Society of Bergen County, New Jersey, from 1956 to 1963. He serves on the editorial boards of *The Humanist* and *Religious Humanism*. He is a consultant to the New Jersey Committee for the Humanities. He has published many articles for various publications and is author of *Toward Common Ground*.

KENNETH J. SMITH is minister of the Unitarian Universalist Society of Martha's Vineyard, Massachusetts. He served as Leader of the Philadelphia Ethical Society from 1962 to 1977. He has been on the executive boards of the United Neighbors, Planned Parenthood, Committee for a Sane World, and the American Civil Liberties Union.

MATTHEW IES SPETTER is leader of the Riverdale-Yonkers (New York) Society for Ethical Culture and is associate professor in social psychology at Manhattan College. He was chairman of the department of ethics at the Ethical Culture Schools for twenty-five years. He is founder of the Riverdale Mental Health Clinic and co-founder of the New York State Commission for the Abolishment of Capital Punishment. He has been a working member of the War Control Study Center since its inception and was a panel participant at the White House Conference on Disarmament. He is also an associate editor of *International Humanism* and the author of three books.